YOUNG STUDENTS

Learning Library

VOLUME 3

Athabascan–Bottle

WEEKLY READER BOOKS
MIDDLETOWN·CONNECTICUT

PHOTO CREDITS

Young Students Learning Library is a trademark of Field Publications.

Copyright © 1990, 1989, 1988, 1982, 1977 Field Publications; 1974, 1972 by Funk & Wagnalls, Inc., & Field Publications.

ISBN 0-8374-6033-6

Contents

ATHABASCAN A group of Indian tribes of Alaska, western Canada, and the western United States speak languages that are all part of the Athabascan (or Athapascan) "language family." These languages are also known as the Na–Dené languages. Athabascan-speaking people settled in North America much later than the very first people who arrived on this continent more than 20,000 years ago. Their ancestors crossed the Bering Strait from Siberia only about 5,000 years ago.

Some tribes who live in Canada—the Beaver, Chipewyan, Ingalik, Hare, Carrier, Dogrib, and Yellowknife—and the Kutchins of Alaska, speak Athabascan languages. Most of these tribes still make a living by fishing, hunting, and trapping. The name "Athabascan" comes from one band of Chipewyans, the Athabascans. The largest group of people speaking Athabascan languages are the Navajo and Apache tribes of the Southwest. The Tlingit and Haida tribes of Alaska and Canada speak a related language.

All Athabascan-speaking tribes use a variation of "the people" as part of all their names. The Navajos call themselves *Dené* (DEE-nay), meaning "the people." The Apaches call themselves *Inde*, which also means "people." Other examples are the Hare Indians who call themselves Kawcho*dine*, meaning "people of the great hares," and the Dogrib Indians, or Thlingcha*dine*, meaning "dogflank people."

During World War II, Navajos serving with the U.S. Marines in the Pacific radioed secret military messages to each other in Navajo. Though behind the battle lines and near the Japanese, they could talk safely, because the Japanese could not translate these messages.

The English language has borrowed a few words from the Athabascan language family. Two borrowed words are *hogan*, from Navajo, and *hooch*, from Tlingit. A hogan is an earth-covered log house, and hooch is a slang word for alcoholic liquor.

ALSO READ: ALGONKIAN; APACHE INDIANS; INDIANS, AMERICAN; NAVAJO INDIANS; TLINGIT INDIANS.

ATHENS Greece's largest city, cultural center, and capital is Athens. It stands on the plain of Attica, between the mountains and the Aegean Sea. Piraeus, its port, is but a few miles away. Athens is one of the world's great historic cities. The art, literature, philosophy, and law of ancient Athens form much of the basis of Western culture and civilization. Today, scholars and tourists come to view remains of the city's ancient history.

Athens was built around a flat-topped hill called the *Acropolis*. This hill was first a fortress to which Athenians fled in case of attack by enemies. Later, beautiful temples were built on the Acropolis in honor of Greek gods and goddesses. The *Parthenon*, one of these temples, is regarded as one of the finest examples of architecture ever built. The public square and marketplace, called the *Agora*, lay beneath the Acropolis. In the 5th century B.C., Athens reached the peak of its cultural achievement.

◀ *Teams of trained life-savers join in the annual parade of Australian life-saving clubs. Australians take great pride in their health and physical fitness. (See* AUSTRALIA.*)*

▲ *A Navajo Indian. The Navajos speak an Athabascan language.*

▼ *The hill of the Acropolis rises above the Greek city of Athens, one of the great historic cities of the world.*

The Atlantic Ocean is slowly growing wider. Scientists have calculated that the distance between the United States and Europe is increasing by about 3 inches (4 cm) a year.

Writers of long ago described the Athenians as people who loved the art of living more than wealth and power. The modern city is much larger than the Athens of old. Its fine public buildings and museums show visitors that Athenians still take pride in their glorious past.

ALSO READ: ACROPOLIS; CITY; GREECE; GREECE, ANCIENT.

ATHLETICS see OLYMPIC GAMES, SPORTS, TRACK AND FIELD.

ATLANTIC OCEAN The Atlantic Ocean stretches from the Arctic Circle to Antarctica. It washes the shores of five continents and is the second largest body of water in the world. The Pacific Ocean is the largest.

North America, South America, Europe, Africa, and Antarctica all border on the Atlantic. Many large gulfs and seas are "arms" of the Atlantic. These arms on the west coast of the Atlantic are Baffin Bay, Hudson Bay, the Gulf of Mexico, and the Caribbean Sea. On the east, the arms of the Atlantic include the Baltic Sea, North Sea, Bay of Biscay, Mediterranean Sea, and the Gulf of Guinea.

The largest islands found in the Atlantic area are in the North Atlantic—the part north of the equator. These include Newfoundland, Greenland, Iceland, the British Isles, Cuba in the Caribbean, and the Azores, west of Portugal. The South Atlantic has fewer islands. The largest southern islands are the Falklands, east of South America's southern tip.

Several *currents* move through the Atlantic. The *Gulf Stream* is the best-known current. It carries warm water north along the east coast of North America and then east to Europe. The *Labrador Current* brings cold water from the Arctic to the shores of eastern North America. The *Brazil Current* flows south along the east coast of South America before turning east.

From the bottom of the Atlantic rise tall underwater mountains. In between the mountains lie deep trenches or valleys. Open plains form islands that sometimes rise above the ocean surface. The *Mid-Atlantic Ridge* is a chain of mountains running from Iceland southward almost to the tip of South America. This ridge is expanding, or spreading out sideways very slowly. Thus, North and South America are slowly being pushed farther from Europe and Africa.

Deep valleys lie on the ocean floor. The *Puerto Rico Trench* is on the

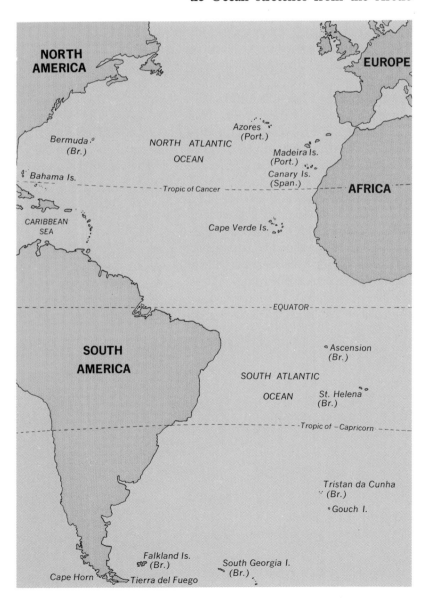

NORTH AMERICA

EUROPE

Bermuda (Br.)

NORTH ATLANTIC OCEAN

Azores (Port.)

Madeira Is. (Port.)

Bahama Is.

Canary Is. (Span.)

AFRICA

Tropic of Cancer

CARIBBEAN SEA

Cape Verde Is.

EQUATOR

SOUTH AMERICA

Ascension (Br.)

SOUTH ATLANTIC OCEAN

St. Helena (Br.)

Tropic of Capricorn

Tristan da Cunha (Br.)

Gouch I.

Falkland Is. (Br.)

South Georgia I. (Br.)

Cape Horn

Tierra del Fuego

The surface area of the Atlantic Ocean is 31,529,000 square miles (81,660,100 sq. km)— more than three times bigger than all of North America.

western edge of the Atlantic Ocean. It is 27,510 feet (8,385 m) deep. Other shallow valleys that look like riverbeds crisscross the wide, flat plains that extend on both sides of the undersea mountains.

The ancient Egyptians were probably the first explorers of the Atlantic. They sailed the Mediterranean and South Atlantic. Later the Phoenicians sailed the Mediterranean past Gibraltar up the North Atlantic to England and Scandinavia. The Vikings were perhaps the first to cross the Atlantic to the New World—a thousand or more years ago. The people who led the way to permanent European settlements along the western Atlantic shore, however, were Christopher Columbus and the explorers who followed him. John W. Alcock and Arthur W. Brown were the first to fly nonstop across the Atlantic, in 1919. In 1927 Charles Lindbergh was the first to "solo" across the Atlantic. Some of today's jet airplanes, such as Concorde, can fly across the Atlantic in less than three hours.

ALSO READ: EXPLORATION; GULF STREAM; LINDBERGH, CHARLES; MAURY, MATTHEW; OCEAN; SEACOAST; TIDE.

ATLANTIS The story of Atlantis comes from the myths of ancient times. Plato, a famous philosopher who lived in long-ago Greece, wrote about this powerful kingdom. He said that Atlantis was a large island in the Atlantic Ocean, somewhere west of the Pillars of Hercules (the Rock of Gilbraltar). Supposedly Atlantis had great armies that invaded many countries around the Mediterranean Sea about 12,000 years ago. Plato said that the ancient Greeks of Athens defeated the armies of Atlantis. Some time after that, giant storms and earthquakes destroyed the island because—the legends say—the people of Atlantis were evil.

Atlantis may never have existed. Its ruins have never been located. But archeologists think it may have been an ancient Mediterranean civilization, flooded after a terrible volcanic eruption. Plato's story could have come from tales that explorers told about real islands they visited in their travels. Someone will perhaps find the remains of glorious Atlantis some day, hidden deep beneath the ocean waters.

ALSO READ: LEGEND, MYTHOLOGY.

▼ *It is thought possible that the Greek island of Thera was once the site of ancient Atlantis.*

▲ *The ancient Greeks told how Atlas carried the world on his shoulders.*

ATLAS A Flemish mapmaker, Gerardus Mercator, was the first to call a book of maps an atlas. In 1585 he named his book of maps after the Greek god, Atlas, because of the old custom of putting a picture of Atlas on the first page of a map book. The Greeks believed that Atlas held the world on his shoulders.

Ancient atlases look strange today. Mapmakers knew little about most of the world's land masses until the 1500's. European mapmakers had to guess at the shape and size of continents other than Europe. They also had very few maps to help them. Maps only began to improve as people explored more and more of the world.

Today's atlases contain many maps. A *world atlas* is usually the biggest type of atlas. World atlases have information about the climate, the natural resources, and the high and low places of each country. The first map in a world atlas generally pictures the whole world. Next come maps of the continents—North America, South America, Africa, Europe, Asia, Australia, and Antarctica. A detailed map of almost every country in the world is included in a world atlas. Each map shows the cities, lakes, rivers, deserts, and mountains of the country. An atlas of the United

▶ *This is the title page from one of the map volumes in Gerardus Mercator's atlas, published in 1585.*

	A	B	C	
1	Lake Erie		Meadville	1
	Cleveland			
2	Akron	Youngstown	PENNSYLVANIA	2
3	OHIO		Pittsburgh	3
	Steubenville			
	WEST VIRGINIA			
	A	B	C	

Akron A2
Cleveland A1
Meadville C1
Pittsburgh C3
Steubenville B3
Youngstown B2

▲ *A page from an atlas with a city gazetteer below to help you locate a city quickly. For example, Akron is in square A2. A refers to the first column of squares down. The 2 refers to the second row of squares across. The point where they cross is square A2, and it is in this square that Akron is located. Can you use the gazetteer to locate Pittsburgh quickly?*

States shows maps of every state in detail. Special atlases may tell about the history of various countries, the products they grow and manufacture, their plant life, or how their boundaries have changed through history. Atlases may have *gazetteers*, lists of names of cities, rivers, mountains, lakes, and deserts, and directions for finding them on the maps.

Countries and cities grow larger or smaller and sometimes change their names. Borders between countries may change through agreement or wars. People who make atlases must constantly bring them up to date. A modern aid to accurate mapmaking is photography, from the air and from satellites in space. This is one reason why modern atlases are better than old ones. An atlas is included in this encyclopedia. Use it when reading articles about countries.

ALSO READ: EXPLORATION, MAP.

ATMOSPHERE Air surrounds the ball-shaped Earth like a transparent shell. This "wrapping" of air is the atmosphere. You could not live without it and the oxygen it contains. It keeps out some harmful rays from the sun. It also keeps the Earth's temperature moderate. The moon, which has no air, has temperatures of 250°F (121°C) during the day and minus 280°F (−173°C) at night!

Although the atmosphere surrounds the Earth, it does not have a definite thickness as the skin of a grapefruit does. It just gets thinner and thinner. It may be divided into four layers. The lowest layer, the *troposphere*, holds most of the air people and other living things breathe. It also provides conditions for weather. The troposphere is not very thick—about 10 miles (16 km) thick over the equator and about 5 miles (8 km) thick over the North and South Poles. But the troposphere has more molecules of air than all the other atmospheric layers put together. Changing conditions in the atmosphere are called weather.

Air is a mixture of gases. Over three-fourths of air is nitrogen, and almost all the rest is oxygen, with tiny amounts, or traces, of other gases. Dust, salt from oceans, pollen from plants, soot from factory chimneys, and ashes from burnt meteors float in the troposphere in the form of vapor, clouds, ice crystals, and rain or snow.

The *stratosphere* is the second layer of the atmosphere. It begins where the troposphere ends and is about 40 miles (64 km) thick. The air is thin and very cold—about minus 67°F (−55°C)—in the lower stratosphere. It is also calm. Jet planes often fly in the lower stratosphere, above wind and rain. In the top part of the troposphere, winds can blow up to 300 miles an hour (480 km/hr). Scientists call these winds *jet streams*.

The third layer of the atmosphere, the *mesosphere*, begins about 50 miles

(80 km) above Earth and reaches upward about 350 miles (560 km). It includes a region that scientists call the *ionosphere*, because it contains many electrically charged particles called *ions*. Air molecules are very far apart in this layer, but they do help protect the Earth from meteors and from strong rays of the sun.

Some important things happen in the ionosphere. Flickering lights sometimes shine there. In the Northern Hemisphere, these lights are called the *aurora borealis*, or northern lights. The southern lights are called the *aurora australis*. Meteors, or "falling stars," start to burn up in the ionosphere, about 70 to 80 miles (113 to 129 km) above Earth. The bottom of the ionosphere reflects (bounces) radio signals back to Earth, enabling messages to be sent around the curved surface of the Earth. Otherwise, all radio waves would shoot off into space.

Above the ionosphere is the *exosphere*, which stretches up hundreds of miles. The higher above Earth you go, the fewer air molecules there are in the same amount of space. In the exosphere the temperature rises again, until it reaches 1800°F (1,000°C).

Outer space is dark, yet when we look up we see blue sky. Why? The answer is that the atmosphere contains many tiny particles of matter which scatter the light reaching the Earth from the sun. They scatter more of the blue light in the sun's light rays than other colors. So we see a blue sky—when there are no clouds low down in the atmosphere to spoil the view.

Other planets and the stars have atmospheres, too. Scientific studies have found that most of these atmospheres probably contain gases different from those in Earth's atmosphere.

ALSO READ: AIR, AURORA, METEOR, RADIO, WEATHER.

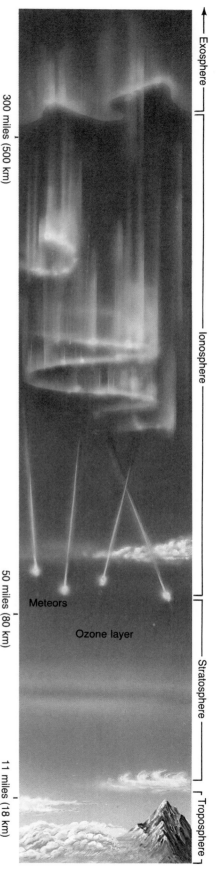

300 miles (500 km)

50 miles (80 km)

Meteors

Ozone layer

11 miles (18 km)

Exosphere

Ionosphere

Stratosphere

Troposphere

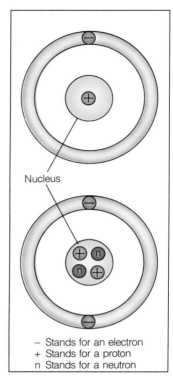

▲ *The nucleus of a* hydrogen *atom* (top) *has one proton. It has no neutrons. One electron revolves around the nucleus. The nucleus of a* helium *atom* (above) *has two protons and two neutrons. Two electrons revolve around the nucleus.*

ATOM Have you ever wondered what would happen if you cut something smaller and smaller, millions of times? Suppose you had a piece of pure gold. You cut it in half, and then cut the half in half. Could you keep on cutting the halves an endless number of times? No. There would come a time when you had a very small piece of gold that could not be cut in half again and still be gold. This very small piece is called an *atom* of gold.

All *matter*, anything that has weight and takes up space, is made up of atoms. The pages of this book and the ink printed on them, a cup and the milk in it, the air you breathe, and all things that can be weighed and measured are made up of various kinds of atoms.

Think of an atom as being round like a ball. If you could put 250 million atoms of average size side by side, they would make up a row one inch (2.5 cm) long. This means that an atom is just one two-hundred-and-fifty-millionth of an inch (11,000 micron) across its widest part or diameter.

There are more than 100 different kinds of atoms. Matter that is made up of only one kind of atom is called an *element*. Atoms of elements combine to make *molecules* of many different kinds of matter. Most elements are found naturally on the Earth, but some have been identified only in laboratories. (See the table of elements in the article on ELEMENT.)

The Idea of Atoms The idea of atoms is not new. Some 2,400 years ago, scientists in Greece wondered what matter was made of. One named Democritus of Abdera believed that all matter was made up of extremely small, entirely solid particles (very small bits) of different sizes and shapes. These tiny particles could not be split or cut, so Democritus named them *atomos*, which in Greek means "not cuttables." Our word "atom" came from *atomos*.

Over 2,000 years later, in 1808, an English schoolmaster, John Dalton, put forward an idea like the one of Democritus. Dalton said that matter was made up of tiny, round solid particles called atoms. His ideas of what atoms were and how atoms behave helped lay the foundation for chemistry.

Inside an Atom We now know that an atom is not solid but is made up of a number of smaller units known as *subatomic particles*. An atom contains a central part called a *nucleus*. One or more *electrons* revolve around the nucleus. An electron is a particle carrying an electric charge. The smallest

▶ *The structure of a* carbon *atom* (atomic weight 6). *The nucleus is made up of protons and neutrons. In a neutral atom the number of protons in the nucleus is the same as the number of electrons orbiting around it.*

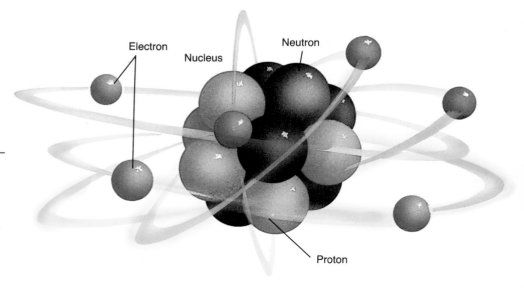

and lightest atom, the hydrogen atom, has one electron. The largest atoms have more than 100. Electrons revolve around the nucleus in orbits that crisscross in several directions, as in the picture. An American physicist, Robert A. Millikan, was able to weigh electrons. He found that each weighed about one three-quadrillionth of an ounce. (A quadrillion is written as 1,000,000,000,000,000.)

The nucleus of an atom is made up of two kinds of particles. A *proton* is a particle with a charge of positive electricity. A *neutron* has no electric charge. (The exception is the smallest and lightest atom, the hydrogen atom. It has no neutrons.)

The weight (or more correctly, the *mass*) of a proton and a neutron are almost equal. The nucleus of a hydrogen atom is more than 1,800 times as heavy as an electron. Although the largest atom has 105 electrons revolving around the nucleus, the combined mass of all these electrons is still a very small part of the total mass of the atom. So the mass of an atom is just about equal to the mass of its nucleus.

The nucleus is very small when compared to the size of an atom. If the diameter of an atom were as long as a football field (100 yards or 91 meters), then the nucleus, on the 50-yard line, would be as big as a pea. So an atom is mostly empty space.

Scientists now know that protons and neutrons themselves are made up of even smaller particles.

Electrons are arranged in orbits in a very definite way. The orbits are called *shells*. The orbit closest to the

◄ *If an atom were the size of your fingernail, your hand would be big enough to hold the Earth!*

nucleus can hold only two electrons. This orbit may have only one electron, as it does in a hydrogen atom. But when the orbit has a second electron, as in an atom of helium, the orbit is said to be *filled*. The orbit next farthest from the nucleus can hold 8 electrons; the third, 18; the fourth, 32; and so on.

Ions and Isotopes   Most atoms have an equal number of electrons and protons. This means that they have the same number of positive and negative electric charges. An atom with equal number of positive and negative electric charges acts as if it had no charge at all. It is electrically *neutral*. But if an atom gains an electron, it will have an extra charge of negative electricity. The atom will be electrically negative. Or, if it loses an electron, it will have more protons than electrons. It will be electrically positive. Atoms that are electrically charged are called *ions*.

When scientists first set about weighing atoms, they decided to say

Scientists keep finding out more and more about the insides of atoms. They now think that everything is made up of tiny particles called quarks and leptons.

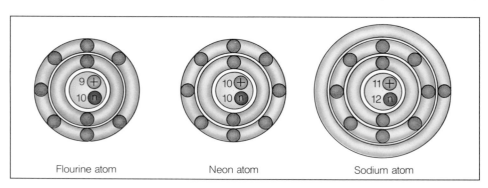

Flourine atom   Neon atom   Sodium atom

◄ *The* fluorine *atom has two shells. But the second shell has only seven electrons and is therefore not filled. The* neon *atom also has two shells. But the second shell has eight electrons and is therefore filled. The* sodium *atom has a third shell, which is only just begun, having one electron.*

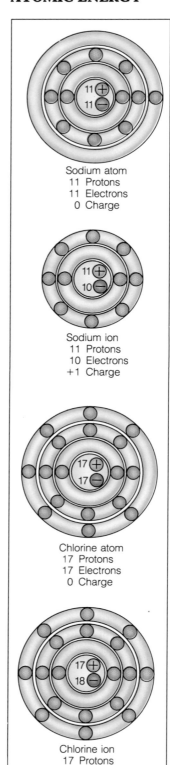

Sodium atom
11 Protons
11 Electrons
0 Charge

Sodium ion
11 Protons
10 Electrons
+1 Charge

Chlorine atom
17 Protons
17 Electrons
0 Charge

Chlorine ion
17 Protons
18 Electrons
−1 Charge

▲ *Atoms become ions when they gain or lose an electron. The diagram shows how the particles of an ion differ from those of a neutral atom of the same substance.*

that an oxygen atom is equal to exactly 16 atomic weight units. They then compared the other atoms to oxygen. (Since 1960, carbon, with a weight of 12, has been used as the base instead of oxygen.) The scientists were puzzled by the fact that the weights of the other atoms were not whole numbers. For example, the chlorine atom has a weight of 35.45. Iron weighs 55.85.

The puzzle was solved when the neutron was discovered. Scientists found that not all atoms of the same element have the same number of neutrons. Chlorine atoms, for example, have two different kinds of nuclei. One contains 17 protons and 18 neutrons, and the other has 17 protons and 20 neutrons. There are 3 times more of the 17-proton-18-neutron atoms than 17-proton-20-neutron atoms. The average of large numbers of the two kinds of atoms gives chlorine its atomic weight of 35.45. Atoms of the same element having different numbers of neutrons are called *isotopes*.

ALSO READ: ANTIMATTER, CHEMISTRY, ELEMENT, GAS, LIQUID, MATTER, NUCLEAR ENERGY, QUANTUM THEORY, SOLID.

ATOMIC ENERGY see NUCLEAR ENERGY.

ATTILA THE HUN (about 406–453) The fierce leader, Attila, and his savage army of Huns from Asia conquered much of the Roman Empire. He was called the "Scourge of God," meaning that he brought punishment.

Attila followed his uncle Roas as king of the Huns, a tribe of nomadic Asians living in what is now Hungary in eastern Europe. Attila first shared the throne with his brother, Bleda, but he later had his brother killed. Attila led his forces from the Danube

▲ *Attila and his Huns terrorized Europe in the* A.D. *400's.*

River to the Mediterranean Sea, killing and burning along the way. Whoever was not killed was forced to serve in Attila's army.

Attila next tried to conquer the Eastern Roman Empire. He could not capture its capital, Constantinople, because of its strong walls. But he forced the city to give him land and pay a large sum of money. Attila invaded Gaul (now France) in A.D. 451. He was stopped by an army of Romans and Visigoths (West Goths) at Chalons, France.

Attila then turned to Italy. He left destruction wherever he went. As Attila neared Rome, Pope Leo I met him and somehow convinced him to turn back. Attila planned to invade Italy again, but he died before he had a chance.

ALSO READ: ROME, ANCIENT.

ATTUCKS, CRISPUS see BOSTON MASSACRE.

AUDIO TAPE see CASSETTE AND CARTRIDGE, RECORDING.

AUDUBON, JOHN JAMES (1785–1851) Birds of all kinds fascinated John James Audubon, and he spent most of his life studying them. He put all the details he observed into beautiful pictures of the birds he studied.

▲ *Audubon's* Blue Jay; *National Gallery of Art, Washington, D.C., gift of Mrs. Walter B. James.*

AUGUST   Long ago the month we call August was called *Sextilis*. It was the sixth month in the ancient Roman calendar. The Roman year began in March. Sextilis was renamed August in 8 B.C., in honor of Augustus Caesar, the first Roman emperor. August is now the eighth month of the year and has 31 days. The poppy and the gladiolus are the flowers of August. August birthstones are the peridot, which is clear green, and the sardonyx, which has brown and white stripes.

August is the peak of the summer in the temperature zone of the Northern Hemisphere. The days are apt to be some of the hottest of the year, though the longest days are past. Hot, sultry days of July and August are called "dog days" by many. This is because Sirius, the Dog Star, rises and sets with the sun and shines very clearly and brightly during August.

▲ *John James Audubon, American naturalist and artist.*

His paintings were made into a set of books called *Birds of America*.

Audubon was born in Haiti. His mother, a Haitian, died soon after his birth. His father, a French naval officer, sent him to France to attend school. Audubon went to live on his father's farm near Philadelphia, Pennsylvania, when he was 18. There he spent most of his time drawing birds. Audubon later opened a general store in Kentucky. But he did not do well in business because he spent most of his time drawing.

Audubon tried to sell his paintings of American birds, but no publisher was interested. He went to England in 1826 and at last published his *Birds of America*. He met William McGillivray, a Scottish naturalist in England. Together, they wrote *Ornithological Biography*, a book about the lives of birds that Audubon painted.

Audubon's work made many Americans aware of their native birds. The National Audubon Society is named in his honor. This organization works to protect birds and to teach people nature conservation.

ALSO READ: BIRD, CONSERVATION.

DATES OF SPECIAL EVENTS IN AUGUST

2 ● President Warren G. Harding died (1923) and
  ● Calvin Coolidge became President.

3 ● Columbus set sail from Spain on his first voyage to the New World (1492).
  ● The *Nautilus* became the first submarine to cross the North Pole underwater (1958).

6 ● United States dropped the first atomic bomb on Hiroshima, Japan (1945).

8 ● The Spanish Armada was defeated by the English Navy (1588).
  ● President Richard Nixon resigned on national television (1974).

9 ● The United States dropped the second atomic bomb on Nagasaki, Japan (1945).

10 ● President Herbert Hoover was born (1874).

12 ● Thomas Edison invented the phonograph (1877).

13 ● Spain captured Mexico City from the Aztecs (1521).

14 ● World War II ended when Japan surrendered to the Allies (1945).

15 ● The Panama Canal opened to traffic (1914).

17 ● Davy Crockett, the American adventurer, was born (1786).

18 ● Virginia Dare was born—the first child of English parents to be born in America (1587).

20 ● President Benjamin Harrison was born (1833).

24 ● The British burned the White House and the Capitol during the War of 1812 (1814).

26 ● Women were given the right to vote by the passage of the nineteenth amendment to the Constitution (1920).

27 ● Confucius, the Chinese philosopher, was born (551 B.C.).

28 ● Great Civil Rights March on Washington, D.C., led by Reverend Martin Luther King, Jr. (1963).

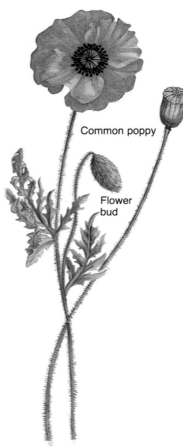

Common poppy

Flower bud

▲ *August's flower is the poppy.*

In far northern Canada and Alaska, chilly nights in August signal the end of summer. In the Southern Hemisphere, warmer winds signal the end of winter in places such as Chile and Argentina.

August is a popular month for taking summer vacations.

ALSO READ: CALENDAR, MONTH, SEASON, SUMMER.

AURORA The night sky in the far north is often bright with dancing lights of many colors. Rays of light shoot across the sky and then fade. "Curtains" of light flicker. This beautiful sight is called the *aurora borealis*, the northern lights. People see similar lights in the sky in Antarctic regions. They are called the *aurora australis*, the southern lights. These spectacular shows may happen at the same time because auroras are caused by the sun and the ionosphere of Earth's atmosphere

When the Italian astronomer Galileo first used a telescope in 1609, he saw black spots moving across the face of the sun. Today, we know that

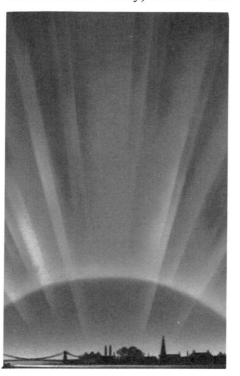

these *sunspots* are huge, violent storms on the sun's surface. Long streams of gas leap from the sun into space during the storms. The gas is made up of tiny particles, and some of them travel to Earth. These gas particles contain electrically charged particles. When the particles are near Earth, they are drawn toward the magnetic poles. The *magnetic poles* are two regions of the Earth, near the North and South geographic poles, that act like giant magnets. When particles from the sun enter Earth's atmosphere, they sometimes collide with other particles that form Earth's air. These collisions make the glow called aurora.

The more storms there are on the sun, the larger the aurora is. Sometimes the glow can be seen in most of the United States. In 1909, an aurora borealis was seen as far south as Singapore, which is almost on the equator! The aurora appears most often in March and April and again in September and October.

ALSO READ: ATMOSPHERE, EARTH, RADIATION BELT, SUN.

AUSTEN, JANE (1775–1817) Jane Austen began writing to amuse herself and her family when she was just a child. She spelled the title of her first book *Love and Freindship*. But her writing—and spelling—improved as she grew older. Years later, she wrote *Pride and Prejudice*, one of the best-known novels ever written.

Jane Austen, daughter of a minister, was born in Hampshire, England. She was the youngest in her family. She never married. Life in the small English towns where her father preached could have been dull, but not to Jane. She was interested in everything and everybody. She often used people she knew as models for the characters in her books. This is one reason her stories seem very real and lifelike. Her books are shrewdly

► *An aurora sometimes forms a bright arch of glowing light in the sky. But most auroras are fainter.*

observed "comedies of manners," written about the daily lives of real people.

Jane Austen wrote six novels. The first one published was *Sense and Sensibility*. It and three others (*Pride and Prejudice, Mansfield Park, Emma*) were published during her life without her name on them because it was not considered respectable for women to write books. Two more (*Northanger Abbey* and *Persuasion*) were published after she died, with her name on them.

AUSTRALIA Australia is a land different from any other place on Earth. Some trees look like bottles. Unusual birds, such as the emu—which cannot fly—and animals, such as the Tasmanian devil—which carries its young in a "pocket" or pouch—are found there. Even the names of towns can be unusual, such as Nowhere Else, Come-by-Chance, or Woolloomooloo.

Australia is the smallest continent and the only continent that is also a single country. Australia's nickname is the "Land Down Under." Find Australia on a globe or world map and see if you can explain why it has this nickname.

The Land Australia is a land of low mountains, beautiful beaches, and a dry, nearly empty interior known as *the outback*. Most people live along the eastern and southern coasts where the climate is comfortable. The east coast is bordered by the Great Dividing Range of mountains. Australia's highest point, Mount Kosciusko (7,316 feet or 2,230 m), is in the southern part of the range. Just to the west of the mountains begins the vast outback, where little rain falls and rivers dry up in the blazing sun. This central region is unsettled except for a few widely scattered mining towns and sheep and cattle ranches known as *stations*. The northern part of the

continent changes from desert to tropical jungle. The south-central part has a number of big lakes. The largest is salty Lake Eyre—the lowest point in Australia. The lake is 52 feet (16 m) below sea level. From the lakes west, the desert extends almost to the sea. The Australian outback will probably always be frontier unless a way can be found to provide water.

The largest coral formation in the world, the Great Barrier Reef, is found off Australia's northeast coast. This beautiful reef extends for more than 1,200 miles (1,900 km). About 600 islands rise from the Coral Sea along the Great Barrier Reef. Heron Island is one of the most interesting. Giant green turtles come to this island once a year to lay their eggs in the warm sand. These turtles are as much as 5 feet (1.5 m) across.

Ayers Rock, in the Northern Territory, is the largest rock outcrop in the world. This natural phenomenon is more than 1,000 feet (300 m) high and 1½ miles (2.5 km) long. The distance around it is almost 6 miles (10 km). The aborigines, the first

▲ *Jane Austen, novelist and observer of English society.*

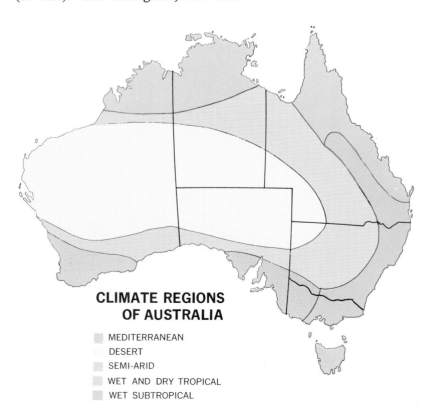

CLIMATE REGIONS OF AUSTRALIA

▨ MEDITERRANEAN
☐ DESERT
▨ SEMI-ARID
▨ WET AND DRY TROPICAL
▨ WET SUBTROPICAL

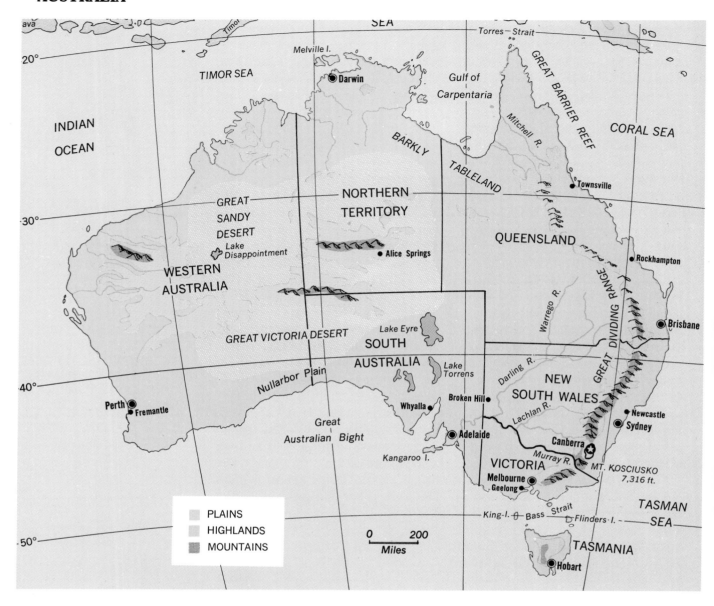

PLAINS
HIGHLANDS
MOUNTAINS

0   200
Miles

AUSTRALIA

Capital City: Canberra (268,000 people).
Area: 2,974,581 square miles (7,704,165 sq. km).
Highest Point: Mount Kosciusko 7,316 feet (2,230 m).
Lowest Point: Lake Eyre 52 feet (16 m) below sea level.
Longest River: Murray River 2,310 miles (3,717 km).

Biggest Lake: Lake Eyre 3,700 square miles (9,583 sq. km).
Largest City: Sydney (3,333,000 people).
Population: 16,000,000.
Government: Federal monarchy.
Natural Resources: Bauxite, coal, copper, gold, iron ore, lead, manganese, oil, opals, silver, tin, tungsten, zinc.
Export Products: Metals and metal ores, cereals, meat, coal, textiles.
Unit of Money: Australian dollar.
Official Language: English.

people to settle in Australia, think Ayers Rock is sacred. Caves in the bottom of the rock are also art galleries of a sort. On the cave walls are paintings and carvings made by ancestors of today's aborigines.

Early History Aborigines from Southeast Asia are thought to have migrated to Australia 40,000 to 50,000 years ago. In the early 1600's, Portuguese, Spanish, and Dutch explorers sighted the continent, but none of them claimed it. A Dutchman, Abel Tasman, discovered an island off the south coast in 1642 and named it Van Diemen's Land (now called Tasmania). The Dutch called the Australian continent New Holland but did not try to settle it. Captain James Cook, an Englishman, landed at what is now Botany Bay in 1770, then sailed north along the east coast, claiming it for Britain as the colony of New South Wales. Colonization had to wait; Britain had the American Revolution to contend with!

The first settlement in Australia came in 1788, at Port Jackson, where the largest city, Sydney, now stands. Captain Arthur Phillip of the Royal Navy was in charge of this strange settlement. Of the first 1,500 settlers, 726 were British convicts. Some, including 180 women, were political

▲ *A vast desert region covers about two-thirds of Australia. Few people live there, because there is not enough rainfall to allow farming.*

prisoners. Many were debtors—people put in jail because they could not pay their bills. More than 160,000 prisoners had arrived in Australia by the time Great Britain stopped sending convicts there, in 1868. Among the prisoners were many talented and able people.

Australia is as large as the United States, not counting Alaska and Hawaii. Australians, like Americans, had to conquer the wilderness before they could build a permanent nation. Settlers formed six colonies—New South Wales, Tasmania, Western Australia, South Australia, Victoria, and Queensland. Each colony governed itself for many years. The six joined together as states of the Commonwealth of Australia in 1901. Two territories—the Northern Territory and the Australian Capital Territory—are also part of the nation.

▼ *Australia's massive sandstone mountain, Ayers Rock, is a sacred aborigine site.*

▼ *This slice across Australia's Great Barrier Reef shows how the land right of the fault line sank. Those parts that remained above water became islands. Other parts were gradually covered by coral, which grew upward to form the world's longest coral reef.*

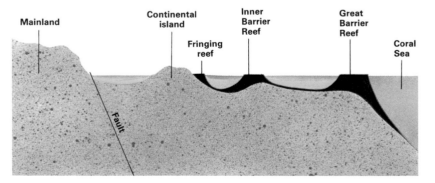

Mainland   Continental island   Fringing reef   Inner Barrier Reef   Great Barrier Reef   Coral Sea

Fault

The Northern Territory is a huge land mass, part desert and part jungle. Very few people live in the Northern Territory. Most work in mines or at remote sheep or cattle stations. The Australian Capital Territory is similar in nature to the District of Columbia in the U.S. Canberra, the national capital of Australia, was built in 1911 on land given by New South Wales. The national government has been established in Canberra since 1927.

Australia Today   Australia is a completely independent nation. It has trade, cultural, and defense links with Britain and the Commonwealth and also has close ties with the United States and with its neighbors in the Pacific and Southeast Asia. The system of government is modeled on the British system. Each state has its own government, but national government rests with the Federal Parliament. National elections must be held at intervals of not more than three years. Parliament is composed of two branches of lawmakers—an upper house called the Senate and a lower house called the House of Representatives. After an election, the leader of the political party or parties that holds a majority of the seats in the House of Representatives is then called upon to form a government composed of Cabinet Ministers. The leader of the ruling party becomes Prime Minister, whose job resembles in many ways that of the U.S. President. Queen Elizabeth II of Great Britain is also Queen of Australia, although she holds no real power. She names a Governor-General to represent her. The real power of the Australian government rests in the hands of the Prime Minister and Parliament.

Two-fifths of Australia's people, nicknamed "Aussies," live in the capital cities of the six states. The capitals and their states are Sydney (New South Wales), Brisbane (Queensland), Melbourne (Victoria), Adelaide

▼ *Sydney, with its famous bridge and opera house, is Australia's biggest city. It has a magnificent natural harbor.*

▲ *An aerial view of Sydney, which is the capital of New South Wales, Australia's most populous state.*

(South Australia), Hobart (Tasmania), and Perth (Western Australia).

Until the end of World War II in 1945, almost every new settler in Australia was from England, Scotland, or Ireland. Since the war, however, thousands of immigrants from other European nations and the United States have been admitted.

In the 1800's, Australia passed strong laws that prevented immigration by non-whites from Asia and Africa. This policy of racial discrimination was criticized by many. In 1973, the government relaxed this non-white policy, and since then Indochinese refugees and other Asians have settled in Australia.

Australian Economy   Australia is the world's top wool exporter. One-third of all wool used in the world comes from Australia. Sheep stations cover thousands and thousands of acres. Large herds of cattle are raised on Australian cattle stations. Agriculture is very important. Besides wool, meat, leather, and dairy products, other major agricultural exports are wheat, cereals, sugar, and fruit.

Fish, oysters, and crayfish are important products of the fishing industry. Divers find valuable pearls in the waters off the coasts. Australia is the world's largest producer of pearl shell—a material used to make buttons and decorations.

Gold mining has been important in Australia since the gold rush in 1851. The finest opals in the world are found in Australia. Diamonds, sapphires, and other precious jewels are also mined. Lead, zinc, tin, copper, and other minerals are mined in Australia, along with huge amounts of iron and coal. There are oilfields in Western Australia and also off the coast of Victoria. The country's leading manufactures are processed farm products and metals, especially iron and steel.

Wildlife Australia split off from the other continents millions of years ago. Thus, plants and animals that have disappeared elsewhere still live in Australia, and new species have developed there. About 400 kinds of animals from prehistoric times live on this continent. The kangaroo is the best known of these. The koala, small and cuddly, is another animal found only in Australia. The duck-billed platypus, an egg-laying mammal with ducklike feet and bill, and the echidna or spiny anteater are curiously "old-fashioned" descendants of early animals. The dingo is a wild dog that the aborigines probably brought when they came from Asia to Australia many thousands of years ago.

Australian birds are also quite unusual. For example, the kookaburra has a strange call that has earned it the nickname "laughing jackass." The emu is a bird 7 feet (2 m) tall. The emu cannot fly. The cassowary bird cannot fly either, but it can run at speeds up to 40 miles per hour (64 km/hr). The lyrebird has an unusual tail that is shaped like a feathered harp. The lyrebird can mimic other birds. Most of Australia's plant life is unlike that of any other continent. Nearly all the trees belong to two groups—acacia and eucalyptus. The acacia grows well in the hot, dry parts of Australia. One acacia species even grows in the desert. The nearly 600 species of eucalyptus grow best in the wetter regions of Australia. But a small species called *mallee* can be found in dry places. Most of Australia has no trees at all—just mile after mile of scrub grass or desert.

Australian Culture Every Australian child must attend school until he or she is 15 or 16. Government trade schools and agricultural colleges are free. Scholarships help students go to college. Some Australian children learn lessons over two-way radio. *The School of the Air* is for children who live too far from towns and cities to attend regular school. These boys and girls live on lonely cattle and sheep stations or in mining camps.

Australia is famous for its athletes. Many great tennis and swimming champions have been Australians. Surfers from Australia are famous wherever the sport is popular. Some of the world's best surf is found along Australian coasts, although sharks are a common danger. Australian sailing crews have proved their yacht-racing skills by winning the famed America's Cup. Few people know that Australia has more snow-covered area than Switzerland. Skiing in the Snowy Mountains compares favorably with that in the Alps or the

The Great Barrier Reef is the largest structure ever built by living creatures. It is made of the remains of tiny creatures called coral polyps. It extends for about 1,240 miles (2,000 km) off the northeastern coast of Australia. It's about as long as the west coast of the United States.

▼ *An Australia sheep station. Wool is the country's chief export product.*

▲ *Australia is the home of unique marsupial animals, such as the wombat (above) and kangaroo. These animals have pouches for their young. When they've grown too large to get inside, the young use these pouches to snuggle in (below). The wombat is a burrowing animal, so its pouch conveniently faces backward and therefore is kept clean.*

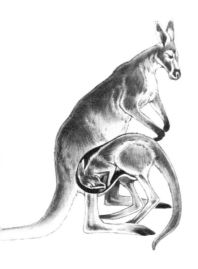

Rockies. Australia, incidentally, had the world's first ski club, formed in 1860. Many favorite sports have come to Australia from Great Britain—cricket, curling, rugby football, and lawn bowling.

Despite its remoteness, Australia has a lively Western culture. Art, music, opera, and ballet are as important "down under" as they are in Europe or the Americas. One of the world's great opera houses can be found in Sydney. The Festival of Arts in Adelaide is world-famous. Melbourne's Moomba Festival is named for an aborigine word meaning "let's all get together and have fun." The Moomba Festival starts in late February or early March. Merrymaking goes on for a week, with many concerts and art shows and a big parade.

Australia is really two places. The big and small cities, where 8 in 10 of the Australians live, have modern buildings and houses and the hustle-bustle common to large population centers elsewhere in the world. Yet thousands of aborigines still live in the outback, though very few of them follow the old hunting way of life. Government reservations have been set up to protect the aborigine culture. Aborigines also work at cattle stations and in offices and factories in coastal towns. They are slowly being accepted as true citizens of Australia. Government aid to the aborigines has been increased and the ownership of sacred sites, such as Ayers Rock (in 1985), is being restored to them.

For further information on:
Animals, see AUSTRALIAN MAMMALS, FLIGHTLESS BIRDS, KANGAROO, KOALA, MAMMAL, MARSUPIAL, PLATYPUS, SHEEP, SPINY ANTEATER, WHALES AND WHALING.
Explorers, see COOK, CAPTAIN JAMES.
International Relations, see COLONY, IMMIGRATION.
People, see ABORIGINE.
Topography, *see* GREAT BARRIER REEF, LAKE, MURRAY-DARLING RIVER.

AUSTRALIAN MAMMALS

Australia has mammals that are found nowhere else on Earth. Most of Australia's mammals are *marsupials,* or pouched mammals. Such mammals give birth to young that need to live for weeks or even months in their mother's pouch until they have grown enough to get along on their own. On the other hand, most of the world's mammals give birth to young already well-developed so they can live safely outside their mother's body. They are called *placental* mammals because the female has an organ called the placenta. It is a network of tissue that helps send food and oxygen from the mother to the growing baby, and it forms when the baby starts to develop in the mother.

The pouched mammals probably evolved (developed) before placental mammals. In most places, the placental animals became powerful enough to take over from the marsupials, most of which died out. However, Australia was cut off by sea from other lands before placental mammals reached there. *Kangaroos, koalas, wombats,* and other pouched mammals were free to develop in Australia without having to compete with the more advanced placental mammals.

Every animal on Earth has a special place and way of life called a *niche.* On different continents, the same niche can be occupied by different animals. Marsupials hold almost every niche in Australia that placental mammals hold on other continents. Placental mammals and marsupials that hold the same niche on different continents may even look alike.

For example, the wolf of the Northern Hemisphere is a chief *predator,* or hunter of other living animals. A now-rare pouched predator, the *Tasmanian wolf* or *thylacine,* lives on the Australian island of Tasmania. In Australia, marsupial "rats," "mice," "cats," and "moles" occupy niches that placental mammals hold in other parts of the world. Kangaroos hold grassland niches of grazing animals, such as deer and antelope. Small marsupials called *phalangers*, including the koala, hold the tree-living niches of squirrels. The roly-poly wombat has teeth and a way of life like that of large placental rodents.

Two other Australian mammals, the *echidna*, or *spiny anteater*, and the *duck-billed platypus*, are also very unusual. Mammals evolved from reptiles, and these two mammals are more closely related to reptiles than any other living mammals. Some of their body parts—the structure of the eye and the shape of the skeleton—are more reptilian than mammalian. More important, these two mammals lay eggs like reptiles but suckle their young like mammals. The young develop and hatch outside the body of the mother.

In South America, some niches were never taken over by placental mammals. Therefore, the pouched mammals that filled them were free to continue their way of life. The *opossum*, which eventually moved into North America, is one of these. Such animals are often called *living fossils* because they have changed very little in millions of years.

ALSO READ: AUSTRALIA, EARTH HISTORY, EVOLUTION, KANGAROO, KOALA, MAMMAL, MARSUPIAL, OPOSSUM, PLATYPUS, SPINY ANTEATER.

AUSTRIA Austria was for hundreds of years the center of a powerful empire that controlled many other European regions. Today, it is a small country in central Europe, about the size of Indiana. Austria is known for its lovely cities, excellent ski resorts, and gracious people. The beautiful Alps extend through Austria from west to east. In the eastern part of the country these mountains open into the Danube Valley, site of the capital city, Vienna. This valley stretches out into a great plain shared by Austria, Czechoslovakia, and Hungary. The Danube River, which flows past Vienna, has long been the main travel route between central and eastern Europe. (See the map with the article on EUROPE.)

One-fourth of all Austrians live in Vienna. This city has many trees and parks and narrow, curving streets. Vienna is known the world over for its music. The city is the home of the famous Vienna Boys Choir, and music lovers from all over the world travel every year to music festivals in Vienna, Salzburg, and Innsbruck.

Several Austrian cities started as Roman army camps, built at the time of Christ. Charlemagne, 800 years later, won control of what is now Austria from the local rulers. The Hapsburgs, a very powerful family in Europe, ruled Austria for 700 years until 1918. Under the Hapsburgs,

Vienna, Austria's capital city, is justly famous for its music and the many composers who lived there. Beethoven, Schubert, Brahms, Mozart, Bruckner, the Strauss family, Mahler, and Schönberg all lived in Vienna. The city is also famous for its coffee houses, where people meet to talk, drink coffee, read the newspapers, and eat delicious Austrian cakes and pastries.

AUSTRIA

Capital City: Vienna (1,500,000 people).
Area: 32,376 square miles (83,854 sq. km).
Population: 7,500,000.
Government: Federal republic.
Natural Resources: Graphite, iron ore, lead, zinc, timber, hydroelectricity.
Export Products: Food, iron and steel, textiles, paper products, machinery, tourism.
Unit of Money: Schilling.
Official Language: German.

▲ *Austria's picturesque alpine scenery attracts many visitors. In winter, mountain villages are busy with skiers and other winter sports enthusiasts.*

Austria ruled one of the most powerful empires in the world, the Austro-Hungarian Empire.

Two world wars ended Austrian power. But Austria has made a comeback and its people live in comfort. Austria has a bicameral legislature and a president who is elected for six years.

The country has much industry. Large waterpower plants produce enough electricity for all of Austria and even for export to Italy and Switzerland. Important products are iron and steel, aluminum, machine tools, chemicals, textiles, leather, wood, milk, butter, and cheese.

More than half of Austria's trade is with the West. It is not a member of the European Community and is generally a neutral in international affairs.

ALSO READ: ALPS MOUNTAINS; CHARLEMAGNE; DANUBE RIVER; EUROPE; HUNGARY; STRAUSS, JOHANN; WORLD WAR I; WORLD WAR II.

AUTOBIOGRAPHY Have you ever kept a diary for a whole year? If so, you have written a kind of autobiography.

A *biography* is a life history of one person written by another. "Auto-" means "self." So, an autobiography is a life history written by the person the story is about. In a diary, a person writes down whatever happens during the day, as it happens. But autobiography writers select certain events in their lives to tell about.

They choose those events in their lives that mean the most to them. They tell their feelings, beliefs, opinions, and thoughts. They may leave out some facts about themselves that are embarrassing or too personal or not important.

Some people write autobiographies that can be very inspiring to a reader, who may learn from the author "not to give up," but to keep on trying to succeed. Helen Keller's book, *The Story of My Life,* is a good example. Miss Keller, who was blind and deaf from infancy, wrote about her struggles as a child to learn to speak and of her final success.

■ **LEARN BY DOING**

Write down what you have done in the past that is important and meaningful to you. What did you think about? What do you think about it now? What interesting people have you met and come to know well? You may be surprised when you read what you have written about yourself! ■

ALSO READ: BIOGRAPHY, DIARY.

AUTOGRAPH An autograph is popularly understood to mean a person's *signature*, the name of a person written by himself or herself. The word autograph comes from a Greek word meaning "self-written." An autograph (also called a *holograph*) is actually anything handwritten by a person—a school paper, an unsigned note, or shopping list.

The more famous the person, the more valuable his or her writing is apt to be. Also, the value is high if the supply of a famous autograph is very small and the demand for it strong. Items signed by William Henry Harrison will most likely be worth more

QUEEN ELIZABETH I

NEIL ARMSTRONG

than those signed by Franklin Delano Roosevelt! They are more scarce, or rare.

■ LEARN BY DOING

You do not need money to collect autographs. You can easily get them from your friends and start an autograph book. And you can often get autographs of famous people, too. You can write letters asking them for their autographs. When some famous person, such as a politican or entertainer, appears near your home, perhaps you can meet them and ask them for their autographs. ■

AUTOMATION Automation seems to be a very complicated process. But really it is just a way of having machines do work without human operators controlling the machines every moment they are running. In other words, an *automated* system is a system that works by itself. Every automated system has two parts—(1) a machine (or many machines) that does the work, and (2) another machine that *controls* the first one.

One automated system in the home is a dishwasher. Inside the cabinet is a machine that washes the dishes, rinses them, and dries them. Also inside the cabinet is a device that "tells" the machine what to do and when to do it. The machine "obeys" the set of instructions. What good

would it do if the machine dried the dishes *before* it washed them?

Your refrigerator is another kind of automated system. Instead of following instructions, it checks how it is working. Inside is a machine that cools the food. This cooler is controlled by a device that checks the temperature inside the refrigerator. If the food is not cold enough, it automatically switches on the cooler.

Some automated systems, like

▼ *In an automated factory, robot machines do repetitive work, such as welding car bodies. Each machine on the line is under the control of a central computer.*

The earliest automation that we know of was invented by Hero of Alexandria in Egypt in the 1st century A.D. Among the many amazing machines that Hero designed was one for opening the temple doors. When a fire was lit on the temple altar, water in a flask was heated. This created pressure that forced water into a bucket. The bucket fell because of the water's weight and pulled a rope that opened the temple doors.

those that make cars, have robots that are controlled by computers. Robot systems are able to perform many different kinds of actions and can easily change from one job to another.

Some kinds of work cannot yet be done by machines. Jobs in which new problems happen frequently, or in which the same actions are not often repeated, are not good candidates for automation. No one has yet built a machine that replaces a doctor. But other jobs, especially repetitive tasks such as calculating sums of money and work on a factory assembly line, can easily be automated.

Automated systems often help people, because machines do work that is boring or even dangerous for people. Jobs such as handling radioactive materials used in nuclear power plants are often done by machines. Automation permits fewer people to manufacture more and better goods, which often means that prices can be lowered.

Automation can also cause big problems. When an automatic system is installed in an office or factory, many workers may lose their jobs. These workers can often get special training to learn new jobs.

The modern world is in an important period of change from machines that need human operators to automated machines. Making a far-reaching change such as this can be painful. People who think that they may lose

their jobs try to fight the change. When the change is more complete, many new kinds of jobs will be available.

ALSO READ: COMPUTER, INDUSTRIAL REVOLUTION, MANUFACTURING, ROBOT.

AUTOMOBILE One invention has done more to change the Western world than anything else. That invention is the automobile. No other discovery in modern history has caused greater changes.

The automobile is the biggest reason why our cities are so huge today. When the centers of cities became too crowded, the automobile took people to the suburbs, but it helped them make the daily trip to jobs in the city. In factories and used-car lots, in oil fields, steel mills, and gas stations, in road building and parking garages, thousands of men and women earn their living from the automobile.

But the automobile has also caused problems. Exhaust fumes add to air pollution. Accidents caused injury and death. In ugly junkyards, old auto bodies pile up. The automobile is a long way from being a perfect means of transportation.

In its short history, the car has come a long way. Not too long ago, most cars were noisy, smelly, uncomfortable, and unreliable. Drivers had to be mechanics. People seldom drove out of town without someone along to fix flat tires, repair the engine, or help push the car out of muddy holes in the road. Going for a ride in an automobile was a real adventure.

Development of the Automobile
The first vehicle that used its own power to move was built by Nicolas Cugnot in Paris in 1769. It was a small, three-wheeled tractor with a steam engine. It sputtered along at 3 miles an hour (4.8 km/hr). Nobody was very impressed, since a person

▼ *Cugnot's steam-powered carriage was meant to pull a heavy cannon. It was slow, but it was the first working automobile.*

can walk that fast. Cugnot's carriage was soon forgotten. The development of self-propelled vehicles began again in Britain in the early 1800's. Unfortunately, the British Parliament thought automobiles too dangerous and tried to stop their use. Parliament passed a law making 4 miles an hour (6.4 km/hr) the speed limit for steam cars. A man also had to walk in front of a "horseless carriage," carrying a red flag during the day and a red lantern at night. This law caused so many problems that for 30 years people stopped experimenting with the horseless carriage. Parliament did not repeal this law until 1896. By then people in Germany, France, and the United States were busy building and driving automobiles.

The *internal combustion engine* gave automobiles all the push they needed to become the fastest-growing industry in the world. This kind of an engine provides power by burning, or exploding, fuel and air inside itself.

Some of today's cars are named for the engineers who first built them. In 1885, Karl Benz of Germany built a three-wheeled car with an internal combustion engine. Today the Mercedes-Benz automobile is famous all over the world. Henry Ford built his first car in 1896. He was one of the first people to understand how important automobiles would be. He helped start the Detroit Automobile Company in 1899. By the next year, 8,000 cars were made in the United States. People were getting used to seeing automobiles on the streets. Henry Ford formed the Ford Motor Company in 1903. By that time David Buick also was building automobiles. Another pioneer automaker, Ransom Olds, built a car he called the Oldsmobile.

A few people, however, still thought steam was better than the internal combustion engine. In almost every town, there were cars like the Stanley Steamer which had a steam engine. Several companies

▲ *Henry Ford cut costs when he put a moving assembly line into his Model T factory. The partly finished cars moved through the factory on tracks, and workers added parts to them as they passed by.*

made cars with electric motors. But the steam engine car was too heavy and too slow, and steam engines often broke down. Electric cars were popular for a while, but they were not really practical because of the short lives of their batteries. The batteries would lose power after as little as 30 miles (48 km). The driver would then have to wait up to six hours for the batteries to get back their power. A long journey in an electric car became a series of short drives and lengthy stops.

The first automakers built one car at a time, just as carriages had been built. This took a long time and cost a lot of money. It also meant that each car was a little bit different from others because the workers made little changes and improvements on every car. All the people in a factory worked together to build one car. When the first car was finished, they started on the next one.

In 1901, Oldsmobiles were built on the first *assembly line*. On an assembly line, car parts were pushed from worker to worker. Each person did the same job over and over. About 5,000 Oldsmobiles were built in 1903 with this new system.

But Henry Ford was the man who really made the automobile so impor-

The electric automobile is not new. At the beginning of this century, about 40 percent of the automobiles in the United States were driven by electricity. Forty percent were driven by steam and only 20 percent by gasoline.

AUTOMOBILE FIRSTS

1860 Etienne Lenoir (Belgium) builds first practical gas-fueled engine

1885 Karl Benz (Germany) builds first automobile

1886 Gottlieb Daimler (Germany) builds first four-wheeled automobile

1892 Rudolf Diesel (Germany) patents engine named after him

1895 Pneumatic tires developed by Michelin brothers (France)

1898 First fully enclosed automobile, Renault

1901 First car with front-wheel drive (France) Ransom Olds begins assembly line production

1908 Henry Ford introduces Model T

1911 First car with electric starter, Cadillac

1913 Moving conveyor belt speeds up Ford assembly line

1916 First car with automatic windscreen wipers, Willys Knight

1919 First traffic lights, Detroit

1928 First car with synchromesh gears, Cadillac

1936 First diesel-engined private automobile, Mercedes-Benz

1939 First automatic transmission, Oldsmobile

1950 First gas-turbine car, Rover (Britain)

1967 Rotary engine, Wankel (Germany)

1972 Instant-seal safety tire, Dunlop (Britain)

1980 General Motors introduce computers to improve engine efficiency

◄ *The Benz three-wheeler of 1885 was the first practical automobile.*

▲ *A 1909 Middleby open two-seater.*

▲ *This 1913 Lancia Theta (Italy) offered passengers more comfort.*

► *1960 Dodge Dart (USA)*

▼ *The sporty and stylish British Jaguar XK120 of 1950.*

A Volkswagen Beetle. This German model was produced from 1938 to 1978.

The British Mini, first produced in 1959.

This 1957 Cadillac was typical 1950's body styling, with huge fins and grilles.

A luxurious U.S. automobile, the Ford Mercury Cougar, 1975.

Streamlined to lessen air resistance, the Lamborghini Urraco (Italy).

Rolls-Royce Corniche, a 1980's continuation of a long line of famous automobiles.

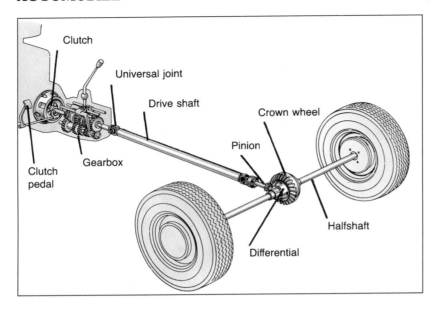

▲ *The automobile transmission system converts the engine's power output to motion to drive the wheels. The system carries enormous strains, particularly in large trucks.*

The United States automobile industry produces over eight million vehicles a year.

tant to life in America. He introduced the Model T Ford in 1908. He improved the assembly line idea in 1913. To the assembly line, he added *conveyor belts*, moving belts that carried car parts from worker to worker faster than ever before. The new Ford system could build six cars in the time it used to take to build one! And it was cheaper. The Model T Ford cost more than 800 dollars in 1908. It cost only 400 dollars when it was built on the new assembly line in 1916.

Henry Ford knew that in order to make and sell many cars, he would have to produce one model at a price that most people could afford. One way he did this was with the assembly line. Another idea he used to build low-priced cars was *standardization*. This meant that each Model T coming from the factory was exactly the same as every other Model T made that year. This process of manufacturing allowed him to produce many inexpensive cars. He would not even paint Model T's different colors. A popular joke of the time was, "You can get a Model T in any color you want, as long as it's black."

Ford was right. His Model T became the best-selling car in the world. Other auto builders took 20 years to catch up with Ford. Americans were driving about 15 million Model T's

by the time the Ford factory started building Model A Fords in 1928.

Moving an Automobile An automobile is a complicated machine. Several things happen when a driver turns the *ignition key*. The key turns on a switch. This lets electricity flow from the car *battery* to a small electric motor. The motor turns a *crankshaft*, a specially-formed bar over and over. *Rods* connected to the crankshaft go up and down as the shaft turns. The rods force *pistons* up and down inside tubes, or *cylinders*. The key turns on the *ignition* (starting) system at the same time. More electricity flows from the battery. First, the electricity goes into a *coil* (loop) that increases its power. Then the electricity goes to a *distributor*. The distributor has one *point*, or switch, for each cylinder. A small rotor (wheel) spins around and touches each point many times every second. Each time a point is touched, electricity flows to that cylinder. A *spark plug* sticking into the cylinder receives the electricity and gives off a powerful spark. This spark causes a mixture of fuel and air in the cylinder to explode. (Gasoline is the most common fuel. Some engines burn liquid propane. Large diesel engines burn heavier oil similar to kerosene.) The explosion of the fuel and air pushes the piston down. The engine is then running. A small *alternator* now takes over for the battery, to produce electricity as long as the engine runs. The battery is used only to start the engine.

But the car still is not moving. To make it move, power from the engine must turn the wheels. That is the job of the *transmission*. Connecting rods and pistons moving up and down keep the crankshaft spinning. The other end of the crankshaft connects to the transmission, or gearbox. The spinning crankshaft turns a gear. The driver chooses this gear by changing the position of a lever near the steering wheel. If gear A is twice as big as gear B, then—when they are turning together—B will go twice as fast as A. The gears are mounted on a *driveshaft*, a straight bar connected by gears to one or both of the car's axles (usually the rear one). When the driveshaft turns, so does the axle. Since the wheels are attached to the ends of the axle, they must spin when the axle turns. The wheels turn faster or slower each time the driver changes gears. Power from the engine is applied smoothly to the driving wheels by means of the *clutch* (a set of discs that are pressed together) or an *automatic transmission*.

The Automobile Today A typical automobile in the United States today has more than 5,000 parts. Many companies make only one or two of these parts, then ship them to an automobile assembly plant. Raw materials that go into making a car come from all over the world. And there are automobile plants in many countries, including Japan, Korea, and Europe. More imported cars are now sold in the United States than ever before.

Today's automobiles come in many different shapes, sizes, and colors. A truck is a kind of automobile, whether it is a giant tractor-trailer truck that hauls loads across the country or a small pickup truck that takes farm products to market. For many years the most popular cars in the United States were large sedans and station wagons that could carry six passengers or more. But the rising cost of gasoline has caused many people to prefer compact cars with smaller engines that get better mileage than those in larger cars.

Automobiles cause about half the accidental deaths in the world. So each year automakers try for improvements in car safety. Padded dashboards, collapsible steering posts, seat belts, and safety bars in doors and roofs are safety equipment that help save lives. Car bodies are made so that in a collision they crumple gradually and absorb much of the force of impact. Improvements in braking systems help drivers to stop quickly in an emergency, without skidding.

The growing numbers of cars and trucks on the roads go on causing traffic jams in busy cities. But the exhaust from cars is becoming less dirty, thanks to clean air laws. Better designs of auto engines are beginning to lessen auto pollution.

■ LEARN BY DOING

How many jobs can you think of that depend on automobiles? You can get some clues from looking in the yellow pages of your telephone book. Suppose that all automobiles suddenly disappeared. In what ways do you think life would be different? ■

ALSO READ: AIR POLLUTION; BUS; CITY; DRIVING; DURYEA, CHARLES AND FRANK; ENGINE; FORD, HENRY; TRUCKS AND TRUCKING.

Three-fourths of the chemical energy of gasoline is wasted when it is used in an automobile.

▼ *One day cars may be driven by electric batteries. The snag is that batteries are heavy, clumsy, and need recharging every few hours. This zinc-nickel oxide battery gives twice the power of a conventional lead-acid battery, so it may be a step toward tomorrow's electric car.*

The world's unofficial one-mile speed record on land is held by Stan Barrett. At the famous straightaway course at Bonneville Salt Flats, Utah, he drove the *Budweiser Rocket* 638.637 miles per hour (1028 km/hr) on October 9, 1979. The official record was broken in October 1983 by British racing driver Richard Noble. He took his car *Thrust 2* up to the speed of 633.5 miles per hour (1019.44 km/hr).

▼ *Grand Prix cars race on special road racetracks. The airfoil "wings" improve the car's road-holding at speed.*

AUTO RACING Auto racing is one of the most exciting and dangerous sports. Each year millions of spectators line roads and racetracks to watch high-powered cars race for fun, fame, and prize money.

There are two main types of auto races—*track races* and *road races*. Track races are run on oval tracks that have straight, flat high-speed sections or *straightaways* and banked or unbanked curves. Road races are run on specially built road courses or on ordinary roads. These courses have sharp curves and hills.

Probably the most famous track race is the Indianapolis 500, run each year on Memorial Day weekend at Indianapolis Motor Speedway. Drivers race at average speeds of more than 200 miles per hour (320 km/hr) around the 2½ mile (4 km) Indy track. The first to complete 200 laps wins the race.

Each year, high-performance racing cars compete in an international series of as many as 16 *Grand Prix* road races, each of which is held in a different country. Every year at least one Grand Prix is held in the United States. Grand Prix cars are known as *Formula One* cars; there are rules governing car design and engine size. Grand Prix races are 150 to 250 miles (240 to 400 km) long. The winner is the first to complete the required number of laps around the course. Points are given to the winner and runners-up. The driver with the most Grand Prix points at the end of the year wins the World Driver's Championship. Other types of cars compete in endurance races, such as the 24-hour races at Daytona, Florida, and at Le Mans, France.

Sports car racing, stock car racing, drag racing, hill climbs, and cross-country rallies are other enjoyable kinds of auto competition. Often the cars are regular production models, specially modified to squeeze the best performance out of them. The Cana-

▲ *A specially modified car speeds through snow during a grueling endurance rally.*

dian-American (Can-Am) Challenge Cup is a well-known race for high-speed sports cars. Another is the Trans-Am series, run by the Sports Car Club of America. In rally driving, cars are driven fast over rough country roads.

Stock car racing attracts many spectators in the United States and Canada. Drivers in *souped up* (supercharged) everyday cars, ranging from jalopies to the latest models, compete on oval tracks (some on road courses). Stock cars are stripped down for lightness. Steel *roll bars* are usually added to strengthen the inside cage of stock cars. Fuel tanks are small in stock cars. Here, as in other auto races, drivers make quick stops at special areas called *pits* to refuel. Tire changes and repairs are sometimes done during *pitstops*.

Drag racing is also popular in the United States and Canada. Souped up cars accelerate (gain speed) from a standing start and race down straightaways. *Dragsters* (drag racing cars) have extra-large, wide rear wheels made of soft, sticky rubber to help grip the track. The fastest dragsters can travel a quarter mile (402 m) in less than six seconds.

ALSO READ: AUTOMOBILE, DRIVING.

AUTUMN Autumn is the season of the year occurring between summer and winter. Americans usually call this season *fall*, the time when leaves on many trees wither and fall to the ground. The leaves of maple and elm trees turn to red and yellow before they fall; brown oak leaves often remain on the trees. And the needle-like leaves of fir trees stay green all year around.

The air in autumn is usually crisp and cool. At night, the harvest moon glows, huge and round. The days grow shorter. In the Northern Hemisphere, autumn begins about September 22, the day known as the *autumnal equinox*. It is one of two days each year when day and night are equal in length. Autumn ends on about December 22, the day of the winter solstice. In the Southern Hemisphere, September marks the beginning of spring, not the beginning of autumn.

A period of warm, mild weather often occurs after the first frost in late autumn. This is known as *Indian summer*; it feels like summer again.

As winter approaches, many birds fly south. Animals such as squirrels, rabbits, and raccoons store food against scarcity during the winter. Other animals prepare to hibernate—bears in caves, bats inside hollow trees, and fish in pond bottoms.

■ LEARN BY DOING

Keep a temperature chart for a few weeks in the autumn. Take the temperature from an outdoor thermometer at home or perhaps one on a bank on your way to school. Write down both morning and evening temperatures. (Indian summers may boost temperatures for a few days.) By the end of three weeks, how have the temperatures begun to change? ■

ALSO READ: HALLOWEEN, LEAF, NOVEMBER, OCTOBER, SEASON, SEPTEMBER, THANKSGIVING, VETERANS DAY.

AVALANCHE A mass of ice, snow, loosened earth, or rock—or a mixture of these—thundering down a mountainside is an avalanche. An avalanche can move down a slope at more than 100 miles an hour (161 km/hr), crushing anything that is in its way.

The simplest kind of avalanche is one of loose snow on the slope of a mountain. If the angle of the slope is steep, the snow is set rolling by any disturbance, such as wind. The mass gathers more snow as it rolls. Such avalanches happen often and are usually not dangerous.

More serious are the slabs of snow that get very deep during winter. Then, on a pleasant spring day, the warmth of the sun loosens the slab and it drops quickly to the valley below. A skier may accidentally set heavy chunks of snow moving and start an avalanche.

Ice avalanches are heavy masses of ice that come loose from glaciers, usually near the bottom where the ice is melted more quickly than at the thicker top. A *rock avalanche*, or *landslide*, may be partly an ice avalanche. If water gets into a crack in rock and freezes, the pressure of the ice can

▲ *Autumn is a time of harvest and natural beauty. The leaves change color, from green to red, gold, and brown, and a blanket of fallen leaves cover the ground. Farmers prepare for winter.*

▼ *An avalanche of snow starts to move. This avalanche was deliberately set moving by firing artillery shells.*

▲ *Aviation pioneers drew pictures of flapping-wing flying machines, like this birdlike ornithopter, designed in 1810.*

▼ *The balloon first took people into the air, beginning with the Montgolfiers' hot-air balloon in 1783.*

break the rock open. It rolls down the mountain, dashing ice or other rocks loose on the way. Earthquakes can also start rocks falling.

A different type of avalanche occurs in areas of steep-sided hills of soil. These avalanches are called *mud slides*. They usually occur after heavy rains when the soil becomes *saturated* (soaked thoroughly) with water. The whole side of the hill flows down the slope like water, destroying everything in its path.

ALSO READ: GEOLOGY, GLACIER, MOUNTAIN.

AVIATION Have you ever wanted to soar high through the air like a bird? Since earliest times, people have wanted to fly. For thousands of years, they were jealous of birds, which flew swiftly overhead while they struggled to walk through jungles, across deserts, and over snow and ice. The human desire to fly is expressed in ancient myths that tell of winged gods and of heroes who traveled the skies in flying chariots. A Greek myth says that Daedalus and his son, Icarus, flew with birdlike wings made of wax, twine, and the feathers of seabirds. Arabian legends tell of people zipping over cities on magic carpets.

People first tried to learn the secret of flight during the Middle Ages. The first experimenters thought they could imitate birds. They made wings, strapped them to their arms, and leaped from high places, flapping as hard as they could. But the human body was not designed for flapping flight, so these would-be "birdmen" crashed to earth. Later inventors designed flying machines called *ornithopters*, which also had wings that could be flapped. But they would not carry a person. A small model ornithopter will fly slowly, in calm air. However, flapping flight was not the answer.

The first truly scientific study of

flight was made in the late 1400's by the brilliant Italian artist and inventor, Leonardo da Vinci. Leonardo realized that human arm and chest muscles are not strong enough to work a pair of wings. But he did design some wing devices that could be attached to both the arms and the legs. He also made detailed drawings of ornithopters, helicopters, and parachutes. The notes and sketches he left show that Leonardo had a good understanding of the principles of flight. But historians are not sure whether he ever built and tested his inventions.

The First Flying Machines The first flying invention to get off the ground was not a flapping-wing machine but a floating machine, a *balloon*. In 1783 two Frenchmen, the Montgolfier brothers, built a huge balloon and filled it with hot air. Because hot air rises, the balloon was able to leave the ground and then float through the air. The Montgolfiers' balloon drifted 5 miles (8 km) in 25 minutes, with two men seated in a basket attached to it. A balloon filled with hydrogen gas, which is lighter than air, was successfully launched later the same year. These early balloon flights must have been exciting, but they were dangerous as well. Besides, they were not very practical because the balloonists could not control the direction in which they floated. They had to go wherever the wind took them. During the 1800's, people tried to guide balloons by using propellers and steam engines. But the engines were too heavy and could not produce enough power.

Inventors meanwhile continued to study the use of winged machines. They had come to realize that fixed wings were better than flapping ones. Many of them built *gliders*, with wings held steady by wires. The glider was an important development in the growth of aviation because it was the first successful heavier-than-air craft. Although it could not really fly, it could coast on air for long distances. Its direction could be controlled by moving parts of the wings and tail, and it could be landed safely. Otto Lilienthal of Germany was one of the great pioneers of the glider. He made more than 2,000 flights during the 1890's.

Other inventors tried adding propellers and lightweight engines to their gliders. These were the first airplanes. In 1886, Clement Ader, a French engineer, built a monster of a plane with huge, batlike wings. Driven by a single propeller connected to a steam engine, it flew only a few feet before crashing. Sir Hiram Maxim of England was even less successful. His steam-powered airplane, tested in 1894, barely got off the ground. An American, Samuel Langley, seemed to be on the right track with his "aerodrome" (meaning "air runner"). But he never got a chance to perfect his plane because he ran out of money.

Two American brothers, Orville and Wilbur Wright, finally came up with the best aircraft of all. They had built and tested many gliders, using different wing designs. They then added a gasoline engine and propellers. Orville piloted the plane on its first successful flight in 1903 at Kitty Hawk, North Carolina. The ancient dream of joining the birds in flight had come true.

Airplanes were soon being built in Europe. France, England, Germany, and Italy made their own models. New designs were tried out to make airplanes more practical, but the early models were still too dangerous to be used for transportation or commerce. Instead, they were used for entertainment and races. Airplanes were new and exciting, and people were happy to pay to see them perform. The first international exhibition was held in Rheims, France, in 1909. Many prizes were offered for the best airplanes and the most skillful pilots. The backers of the exhibition ex-

pected about 50,000 people. But more than 250,000 attended. The success of this and other air meets led airplane makers to build better models in order to win more prizes and attract bigger crowds.

Daredevil pilots called *barnstormers* traveled all over the United States to perform thrilling stunts at carnivals and county fairs. They raced with automobiles and other airplanes. They walked on the wing of a plane in flight or hung by their hands or knees from the landing gear. They picked up handkerchiefs off the ground with a hook on the tip of the wing. Sometimes they dropped candy and flowers to the cheering crowd below. Some of the more daring members of the audience would pay for a private ride after the show. Barnstormers were often paid a great deal of money for their amazing stunts. They led dangerous lives, and many were killed. But they helped to introduce aviation to the American public.

▲ *The first motor-powered flight in a heavier-than-air machine in 1903. In the Wright brothers' Flyer 1, Orville Wright flew for 12 seconds, covering just 120 feet (37 m).*

▼ *Biplane (two-wing) aircraft were the type most used in World War I (1914-1918). This is a British Sopwith Camel fighter.*

▲ *The P-51 Mustang was the best long-range fighter escort of World War II (1939-1945) and one of the last propeller-driven warplanes.*

The airplane became a weapon of war when World War I started in 1914. The warring nations of Europe wanted as many planes as they could get, to use for observation, bombing, and other purposes. Small companies that had been building planes slowly, by hand, began to speed up production. They hired the best scientists and engineers.

Modern Aviation Since World War I, rapid progress has been made in aviation. Regular airmail service between New York and Washington began in 1918. Coast-to-coast service was first offered in 1924. Spectacular record-making flights—such as Charles Lindbergh's solo crossing of the Atlantic Ocean in 1927—proved the power, speed, and safety of the airplane. During the 1930's, commercial airlines for carrying passengers and cargo began in Europe and America, and the first practical helicopter was developed.

World War II brought even greater advances in aviation, with the coming of the jet age—though only a few jet planes were flown in action. By the late 1950's airlines were using jet airliners, such as the Boeing 707. More and more people took to the air, and holiday travel by air became big business worldwide.

The 1970's saw the introduction of the world's first commercial faster-than-sound airliner, Concorde. And the 1980's brought a new kind of airplane, the Space Shuttle. The Shuttle can fly like a spacecraft in space, but glide back to land on the ground, like a plane. The latest airliners are much quieter and use less fuel than older types. Computers help engineers build more efficient airplanes than before.

The aviation, or aerospace, industry is the second largest in the United States (after automobile making). Aircraft have many uses, and there are many different types—from the small, slow planes used for crop-dusting to the supersonic jets of the Air Force. So big is the Boeing 747 jumbo jet that the Boeing Company built the world's largest building outside Seattle, Washington, as a factory for making the huge planes. Millions of people are employed in the aerospace industry.

ALSO READ: AIR FORCE; AIRLINE; AIRPLANE; AIRSHIP; BALLOON; GLIDER; HELICOPTER; JET PROPULSION; LINDBERGH, CHARLES; WRIGHT BROTHERS.

▼ *How aircraft speeds increased after World War II. The speed of sound, or Mach 1, is 760 mph (1,223 km/hr) at sea level. Higher up, sound travels more slowly. So at 36,000 feet (11,000 m) Mach 1 is only 660 mph (1,062 km/hr).*

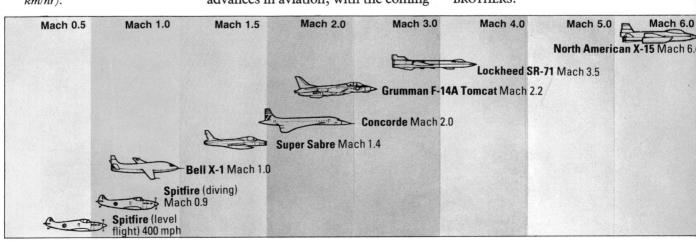

| Mach 0.5 | Mach 1.0 | Mach 1.5 | Mach 2.0 | Mach 3.0 | Mach 4.0 | Mach 5.0 | Mach 6.0 |

North American X-15 Mach 6.

Lockheed SR-71 Mach 3.5

Grumman F-14A Tomcat Mach 2.2

Concorde Mach 2.0

Super Sabre Mach 1.4

Bell X-1 Mach 1.0

Spitfire (diving) Mach 0.9

Spitfire (level flight) 400 mph

▲ Propeller-driven, piston-engined planes, like this Cessna, are widely used for private business and sports flying.

▲ A sailplane or glider. These airplanes have no engines and gain height by seeking upward-rising currents of air.

▲ The Bell X-1, piloted by Charles Yeager, was the first aircraft to break the so-called "sound barrier," in 1947.

▼ The helicopter is a versatile aircraft. This is a U.S. Navy Seasprite, used for anti-submarine patrols at sea.

▲ A small executive or military jet can land at small airfields that big airlines do not serve.

▶ Concorde, the only supersonic airliner in service, cruises at 1,200 mph (2,000 km/hr) and carries up to 140 passengers between Europe and the United States.

An Aztec warrior's chief aim in battle was to take as many prisoners as he could and hand them over to the priests for sacrifice to the gods. It is believed that the Aztecs often used to eat the bodies of their victims.

AXIS see GRAPH, SYMMETRY.

AZTEC INDIANS The Aztec Indians created a great civilization in Central Mexico that reached its peak in the early 1500's. About A.D. 1200, the Aztecs settled in the Valley of Mexico, where Mexico City stands today. (See the map with the article on INDIANS, AMERICAN.) The Aztecs dug canals and drained marshes to make farmland. They heaped mud into huge, woven-reed baskets and sank the baskets to the bottom of shallow lakes to make artificial islands. They planted trees on these islands, and the trees took root in the bottom of the lakes. In time, the islands became farmlands.

Corn was the main crop of the Aztecs. The women made a coarse corn meal by grinding corn between two stones. They made flat cakes, called *tortillas*, out of this coarse meal. The Aztecs also grew avocados, beans, chili peppers, cotton, squash, tomatoes, and tobacco.

Not long after the Aztecs settled in the Valley of Mexico, their warriors conquered neighboring tribes and formed an empire. About 1325, the Aztecs began to build a capital city. They called it *Tenochtitlan*. The people built houses out of mud and twigs woven together. They thatched the roofs with grass. Canals ran between farms and continued into the city. Up and down the canals, Indians in dugout canoes hauled their produce to market. Tenochtitlan became a splendid city, with gardens and a zoo. The Aztecs were skillful stone carvers and artists. They loved jewels and decorated pottery.

In the city's main plaza stood several huge terraced pyramids. Atop each pyramid stood one or two temples to Aztec gods. Religion was very important to the Aztecs. They depended on forces of nature—the sun, rain, and wind—to help them grow crops, so the Aztecs worshiped these forces as gods. They believed that "good gods," such as the sun god, had to be kept strong. The good gods could prevent certain bad gods from taking control and ruining the lives of the people. They believed that one way they could keep a good god strong was to feed him human hearts and blood. Each year Aztec priests sacrificed many young men to the gods. One year, about 50,000 prisoners of war were killed.

Hernando Cortés, a Spanish explorer, led more than 500 Spaniards into Mexico to search for gold in 1519. At first the Aztecs believed Cortés was the representative of a white-skinned god, so they respected him. Then he angered them by melting down their gold ornaments and shipping the gold to Spain. A young Aztec named Cuauhtemoc led the people against the Spaniards, who were forced to retreat. Cuauhtemoc became emperor of the Aztecs when his uncle, Emperor Montezuma, was killed by the Spaniards in 1520. Cuauhtemoc again led his people when Cortés and his men returned to attack Tenochtitlan. But the Aztecs' war clubs could not overcome the Spaniards' muskets. The Spaniards killed the young emperor and completely destroyed the capital city in 1521. They built Mexico City on its ruins.

ALSO READ: CORTÉS, HERNANDO; INDIAN ART, AMERICAN; INDIANS, AMERICAN; MEXICO; MEXICO CITY.

▶ *An Aztec mask. The Aztecs were skillful artists and builders.*

BABBAGE, CHARLES (1792–1871) It often seemed to Charles Babbage that his life was nothing but a complete failure, but today he is regarded as a genius. He was a British inventor and mathematician, and one of his inventions was the first modern computer, which he called an "analytical engine." Babbage had the idea for this in 1834. But his computer was never completed. It would not have worked even if it had been, because its levers and gears could not be made accurately at that time. However, in planning it, Babbage worked out many of the principles of modern computers. He planned to use punched cards to feed in information and instructions, and he worked out ways for the machine to store the results of sums in its "memory" so that those results could later be used to solve more complicated sums. His partially completed "analytical engine" is in London's Science Museum today.

In 1847 Babbage invented an *ophthalmoscope*, a device to let doctors

◀ *Charles Babbage worked out the principles of the computer but could never build his "Analytical Engine." A model of it* (below) *was made later from notes Babbage left.*

look at the retinas of patients' eyes, but the doctor to whom he lent his model for testing forgot all about it! A few years later a German named Hermann von Helmholtz invented a similar device, which was a success. Near the end of his life Babbage tried to invent a way of always placing winning bets on horse races, but again he was unsuccessful.

ALSO READ: COMPUTER.

▲ *An enameled painting on brick of two musicians. The brick was made at Ur, at one time a very powerful city in Babylonia.*

BABYLONIA The Babylonians lived thousands of years ago in the ancient land of Mesopotamia, now called Iraq. But the first civilized people to live there, around 6,000 years ago, were *Sumerians.* Sumer was conquered by Akkadians, over 4,000 years ago, and the land was called *Sumer and Akkad.* Later on, about 1720 B.C. a Babylonian king named

▼ *Babylon and its surrounding lands formed a flourishing cradle of civilization. Shown on the map are three symbols of Babylonian civilization: a tablet of cuneiform writing, the Ishtar Gate, and one of the reed ships that Babylonian traders sailed to Egypt and India.*

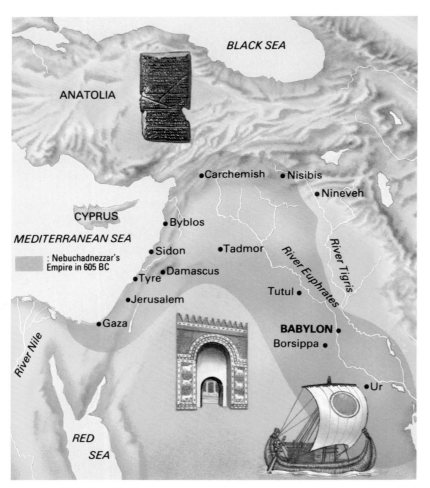

Hammurabi conquered other kingdoms around Babylonia and built an empire. He ruled well, but his empire weakened and was taken over by Assyria. Then another king, Nebuchadnezzar, started another strong empire and made Babylon his capital city. He built many magnificent temples there.

The Babylonians were good farmers with fine *irrigation,* or watering, systems, an idea that they borrowed from the Sumerians. They knew about surveying land, engineering, astronomy, medicine, and astrology. They used the 60-minute hour and the 24-hour day to tell time. Of their many works of art, two famous stories are the *Creation Story* that tells about the world's creation by Marduk, the sun god of Babylon, and the *Gilgamesh epic* that describes a flood similar to that in the Bible. *The Code of Hammurabi* was a system of law that covered every part of daily life. In the city of Babylon were the famous *Hanging Gardens,* one of the Seven Wonders of the Ancient World, and many pyramid-shaped towers called *ziggurats.* One of them may have been the "Tower of Babel" described in the Bible.

The Babylonians believed that there were as many as 4,000 gods. Everyone had his or her own personal god. People lived by the rules of justice, law and order, courage, kindness, and truth. In 539 B.C., the country was taken over by the Persian Empire, and then conquered by Alexander the Great. Babylonia never again regained its independence or its lost glories. The ruins of ancient Babylon still exist in modern Iraq.

ALSO READ: ANCIENT CIVILIZATIONS, ASSYRIA, MESOPOTAMIA, SEVEN WONDERS OF THE WORLD, SUMER, TIME.

BACH FAMILY Many fine musicians came from the talented Bach family of Germany. At least 50 Bach family members were musicians in the 17th and 18th centuries. One of them, Johann Sebastian, was one of the greatest composers of all time.

The first member of the family whom we know about was Veit Bach, a baker who died in 1619. Veit liked music, and his son, Hans, was a fiddle player. All of Hans's sons became musicians. Soon, many Bachs were musicians in churches and in the courts of noblemen. If one died or moved away, an uncle or cousin often replaced him.

Johann Sebastian Bach (1685–1750) was born in Eisenach, Germany. His father was Johann Ambrosius, great-grandson of Veit. Johann's parents died when he was ten years old, and he lived with his older brother. Johann learned the harpsichord at this time. He won a scholarship as a choirboy when he was 15, and he studied voice and organ music. He held several teaching positions and then moved to Leipzig, Germany, in 1723, where he stayed for the rest of his life. He worked as teacher, organist, and music director at St. Thomas's School and Church.

Bach wrote music all during his life, but almost none of it was performed while he was alive. He won honor as a musician, but not until long after he died did the world acclaim him as a great composer. Musical interest for almost 100 years took a turn away from the kind of music he had written. Bach's works for chorus and orchestra include *The Passion According to St. John*, *The Passion According to St. Matthew*, the *Christmas Oratorio*, and the *Mass in B Minor*. He also wrote hundreds of other pieces for keyboard, organ, and orchestra. Many of them are in the embellished style called *Baroque*, with different melodic lines going on at the same time, and passages in which musicians were encouraged to ornament the melody with trills and other notes they might improvise.

Bach married his cousin, Maria, in 1707. They had seven children before she died in 1720. Bach married Anna Wilcken the next year, and they had 13 children. Two of Bach's sons, Karl Philipp Emanuel (1714–1788) and Johann Christian (1735–1782), were also famous composers.

ALSO READ: BAROQUE PERIOD, CHORAL MUSIC, COMPOSER, MUSIC, ORGAN.

BACON, FRANCIS (1561–1626) Sir Francis Bacon was an important English statesman and philosopher. He was born in London and went to Trinity College in Cambridge. He served King James I as Attorney General, as Lord Chancellor, and as chief minister of state. Bacon often gave very good advice to King James, who knighted him. But while Bacon was Lord Chancellor, he was found guilty of taking a bribe—accepting money for a dishonest favor. He was sent to the Tower of London, a prison for important people. The king finally let him out of jail, and Bacon spent the rest of his life writing.

He often wrote about honesty, truth, love, and friendship. His greatest contribution was in writing about

▲ *Johann Sebastian Bach, most famous member of a family of musicians.*

▲ *Sir Francis Bacon, English statesman and philosopher.*

Francis Bacon said that three inventions had changed the world. They were printing, gunpowder, and the compass.

▲ *Roger Bacon, English scientist and philosopher.*

▼ *Bacteria can reproduce very rapidly. In good conditions, a single bacterium could leave 280,000 billion descendants after 24 hours.*

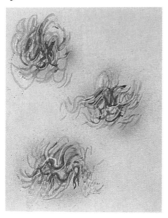

After 6 hours

After 9 hours

the scientific method. He helped improve science by telling scientists to observe—to study carefully—the things they wanted to explain. Some people think that Bacon wrote the plays of Shakespeare, but most experts disagree. The books and essays that Bacon did write are still read by people all over the world.

ALSO READ: SCIENCE.

BACON, ROGER (about 1220–1294) Roger Bacon was a medieval scientist and experimenter. He was so clever that he was accused of being a magician.

Very little is known about his life. He was born in Ilchester, England, and studied at Oxford University. He taught in Paris for a time and returned to Oxford about 1251. He took up a broad study of languages, mathematics, logic, and science—including astronomy, alchemy, and optics (the study of light and vision). But about 1257 Bacon became a Franciscan monk and some of his ideas got him into trouble with the other monks.

Pope Clement IV heard of Bacon's ideas and secretly asked him to write a book on the sciences. Bacon wrote *Opus Majus* ("Great Work"), an encyclopedia of the scientific knowledge of his day. He was later put in jail for a time but managed to write two more scientific books.

Bacon was the first known European to write about gunpowder. He predicted automobiles, submarines, frozen foods, balloons, and a sort of airplane with flapping wings. Most important was his belief that people can learn more by experience and reason than from merely following old ideas. He taught others to gain knowledge by experiment and not to accept old beliefs without question.

ALSO READ: ALCHEMY, ASTRONOMY, SCIENCE.

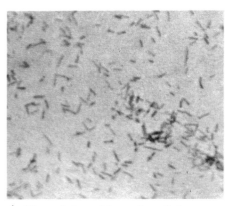

▲ *The rod-shaped bacteria called* Salmonella *(that can cause food poisoning). The photograph was taken through a microscope because bacteria are too small to be seen with the naked eye.*

BACTERIA Bacteria live in air, in water, in soil, in most food and drink and in the bodies of animals and plants. Bacteria (singular is "bacterium") are tiny single-celled organisms. Some bacteria can move about, so scientists once thought they were animals. It was then found that unlike animal cells, bacteria's cells have firm walls. So they were called plants. But now scientists call bacteria (and some other tiny organisms) *protists*—not animals or plants, but with features of both.

Bacteriologists (biologists who study bacteria) place these tiny living things into three main groups according to their shapes. Rod-shaped bacteria are called *bacilli*. Ball-shaped bacteria are called *cocci*. And spiral bacteria are called *spirilla*. These living things are so tiny that it would take as many as 50,000 of them to cover one square inch (6.4 sq. cm).

Each bacterium is a single cell. It contains protoplasm and is enclosed by a firm layer (cell wall). Many bacteria can move about by means of *flagella*, tiny hairlike threads. Other bacteria do not have flagella and must be carried about by wind, water, or other means.

Bacteria reproduce by simple *fission* (division). One cell splits into two, and two into four, and so on. A mass of bacteria is called a *colony*. One bacterium could produce about three billion more bacteria—or as many people as there are in the world—in less than a day if none of the cells died. Fortunately, many cells die.

Some bacteria die if they are dried out. Others die when they are cold. Heat kills bacteria, but some kinds of bacteria form hard covers and become *spores*. These bacteria can live for several hours even in boiling water.

Some bacteria need oxygen. But others, called *anaerobic* bacteria, die if they come into contact with oxygen. Bacteria that live freely in oxygen are *aerobic*. Bacteria feed on organic matter. *Saprophytes* eat dead animals and plants. Dead organisms would pile up and take the room that living things need if it were not for these bacteria. Bacteria that live within living animals and plants and harm them while getting food from them are *parasites*. Other bacteria can make some of their own food from inorganic substances.

Some bacteria cause serious diseases, including cholera, tetanus, tuberculosis, leprosy, scarlet fever, diphtheria, and some types of pneumonia. Bacteria may act in three ways: (1) by *direct action* to destroy tissues, as in tuberculosis; (2) by *mechanical effects*, as when a clump of bacteria blocks a blood vessel; and (3) by producing chemical poisons or *toxins* as in typhoid fever.

In 1880, Louis Pasteur, a French scientist, discovered that if weakened or dead bacteria are injected into animals, the animals are able to resist diseases caused by these bacteria. This discovery led to the prevention of many diseases by *vaccination*.

Most bacteria are not harmful. In fact, life could not continue without many kinds of bacteria. Bacteria that live in soil cause dead plants and animals to *decompose* (break down) into the chemical elements of which they are made. The process of decomposition frees nitrates and other important substances used by living plants—and the animals that eat the plants. The cycle of life goes on when those organisms die.

Other useful bacteria live in the digestive systems of people and animals. Bacteria in the stomachs of grass-eating animals break down *cellulose*, the material that forms the stiff walls of plant cells. The work of such bacteria allows cows to digest grass, one step in the production of milk. Other bacteria can ferment the milk, a necessary process in making cheese, butter, buttermilk, and yogurt. Still other bacteria are used to soften the plant fibers from which thread is spun, to tan hides in leather making, and to eat away the shells of coffee and cacao beans. Some bacteria may stop the harmful bacteria that cause cavities in teeth, for example. And other kinds of bacteria may even be nutritious food. Some bacteria can be altered in the laboratory so they produce useful substances such as medicines.

ALSO READ: CHEESE; CHILDHOOD DISEASES; CONTAGIOUS DISEASES; DISEASE; HERBIVORE; IMMUNITY; PASTEUR, LOUIS; PLANT DISEASES; PROTIST.

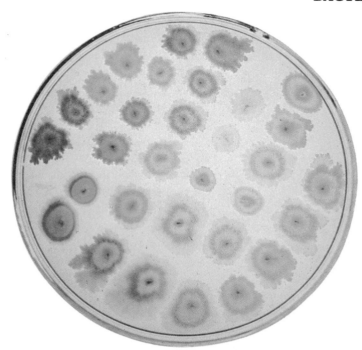

▲ *Colonies of the bacterium* Bacillus subtilis *can be used as "factories" for making particular products. The red colonies are the best producers. White colonies are non-producers.*

▼ *Bacteria come in different shapes. Some are round, some are rod-shaped, while others look like spiral corkscrews.*

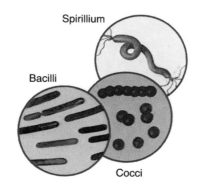

Spirillium

Bacilli

Cocci

BADEN-POWELL, ROBERT
see YOUNG PEOPLE'S ASSOCIATIONS.

BADGER see WEASEL.

BADLANDS A rough, barren wilderness, about the size of Delaware, lies in southwestern South Dakota near the Black Hills. Indians gave it a name that meant "the Badlands." If you go there, you can stand atop a hill and gaze at mile after mile of jagged ravines and pointed rocks. After sundown, the moonlight casts harsh shadows across the land.

Rain in the Badlands usually comes as heavy downpours. For centuries, the water has washed loose dirt and rock down from the Black Hills. The material has collected in the low land below the hills. Storms and streams cut weird gullies through the soft clay and sandstone. Continuous erosion has deepened these gullies. Blue, pink, green, and tan minerals add color to the basically gray rock.

Prairie dogs, cottontail rabbits, and coyotes live on the edges of the Badlands. Much larger animals lived there about 24 million years ago. Fossils of saber-toothed tigers, rhinoceroses, and three-toed horses have been found preserved in the clay.

ALSO READ: EROSION, SOUTH DAKOTA.

▼ *The Badlands of South Dakota form a landscape of many different colors and shapes.*

BADMINTON Badminton is a game that is like tennis in some ways. The players use *rackets* to bat an object over a net. The game is played on a *court*, although a badminton court is smaller than a tennis court. The net is strung between two poles, with its top 5 feet (1.5 m) above the ground. Badminton is often an indoor sport but can be played on a lawn if there is no wind. It can be played by two people (*singles*) or four (*doubles*).

A badminton racket is smaller and lighter than a tennis racket. The handle is slimmer, and the head is much smaller. A lighter racket is used because the badminton player must be able to make shots very quickly with a snap of the wrist.

The game is played by *volleying* (hitting) a *shuttlecock*, called a "bird," over the net without letting it touch the ground. The shuttlecock or bird is a small cork hemisphere with a bunch of feathers (real or more usually plastic) attached.

Only the side serving the bird can

▼ *Badminton is played indoors and out. It is an enjoyable and energetic game for two or four players.*

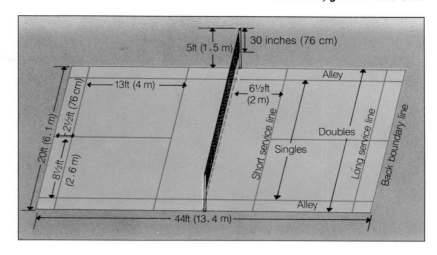

score a point. When the opponent allows the bird to touch the ground, hits it out of the playing area or into or under the net, or allows himself to be touched by the bird, the serving side is awarded a point. The first side to score 15 points wins the game.

Skillful players can control the bird and place their shots. They can lob the bird behind the opponent, drop it gently just over the net, or smash it straight past the opponent at a surprisingly fast speed.

Badminton was first played in India centuries ago. It was then called *poona*. Army officers brought the game to England about 1870. It was played at a party on the estate of the Duke of Beaufort in 1873. The estate was called "Badminton." The sport quickly spread to America and elsewhere.

ALSO READ: SPORTS, TENNIS.

BAGPIPE Musicians played the strange instrument called the bagpipe long before Christ was born. The Roman Emperor Nero played the ancient instrument, and the Roman army probably marched through Europe to its music. The bagpipe was popular all over Europe in the Middle Ages. Today, people in Ireland, France, Spain, and India play the bagpipe. But it is known chiefly as the national instrument of Scotland.

A Scottish bagpipe consists of a bag, usually a sheepskin, and several reed pipes. The player blows into the *blowpipe* and fills the bag with air. As he continues to blow, the air is forced into the melody pipe, or *chanter*. To play a tune, the player puts his fingertips over holes in the chanter. Air is forced into several other pipes, too. These are called *drone* pipes. Most bagpipes have three drone pipes, each of which produce a different, continuous note. The drone notes make a background for the melody.

The bagpipe produces a strange,

shrill tone, called a *skirl*, which often led Scottish armies into battle. Bagpipes are also used to play *pibrochs*, traditional songs with many variations, and music for folk dances such as the "Highland Reel."

ALSO READ: MUSIC, MUSICAL INSTRUMENTS, SCOTLAND.

BAHAMAS see WEST INDIES.

BAHRAIN see ARABIA.

BAIRD, JOHN LOGIE (1888–1946) John Logie Baird was a Scottish inventor and one of the pioneers of television. He was born in Helensburgh, Scotland, and he attended the University of Glasgow. In 1922 Baird began to think about *transmitting* (sending) pictures across great distances. Using a mechanical system (rather than the electronic system later adopted as standard), Baird transmitted the first crude television pictures in 1924. These pictures showed only the outlines of objects. But Baird quickly developed his new invention. He was soon able to send clear TV pictures of human faces. He gave a public demonstration of the first true television at the Royal Institution in London, on January 27, 1926.

▲ *A Scottish piper wearing national costume.*

▼ *John Logie Baird with a dummy he used to test his pioneer television equipment.*

▲ *Baird's 30-line "televisor" of 1930 came four years after he successfully demonstrated television. In the end, however, Baird's system lost out to the rival electronic system invented by Vladimir Zworykin.*

The longest loaf of bread ever baked was 100 feet (30.5 m) long. It was baked in 1969 in Auckland, New Zealand.

He also invented a "noctovisor," for seeing in darkness and through fog, using infrared light. Baird transmitted his first color picture in 1928, and developed clear, brilliant pictures in natural color by 1939. He devoted the last years of his life to trying to discover how to transmit three-dimensional television pictures.

ALSO READ: TELEVISION; ZWORYKIN, VLADIMIR.

BAJA CALIFORNIA   see MEXICO.

BAKING AND BAKERIES Bread was the first food to be made, rather than gathered. People all over the world have been bread bakers for thousands of years—long before written history. Until the 20th century, most people baked their own bread at home. The first breads were probably made of nuts or wild grass seeds pounded between two stones. People slowly learned to farm, and they raised large crops of grain—wheat, rye, millet, barley, oats, and corn—for bread. People learned to change the taste and texture of grain by changing the way it is *milled* (ground). Milling separates the *flour*,

or food part of grain, from the *bran*, or seed coat. Millers today can make about 150 different flours by changing the grinding process.

Early bread was not like the bread you are probably used to. It was flat, heavy, and dry. It looked and tasted something like Mexican tortillas. Archeologists have found a piece of such bread over 4,000 years old in the ruins of an ancient village in Switzerland.

The bread that people eat most often today is baked from *fermented* dough, which contains bubbles of carbon dioxide, a gas. The bubbles expand when the dough is heated, and the bread *rises*—becomes light and airy. Dough ferments if it stands before it is baked. But this takes a long time, so bakers often add *yeast*, a tiny plant that releases carbon dioxide into the dough. It speeds up the *leavening* (rising) process. The ancient Egyptians probably discovered this by accident when some yeast cells were blown through the air and landed on unbaked dough. The process of *kneading* (folding, pressing, and stretching dough with the hands) is often required for breads made with yeast. Some modern yeast breads are coffee cakes, yeast rolls, and sweet breads.

Bakers sometimes add baking powder, baking soda, or both, to dough—instead of yeast. Such dough rises as it bakes, so it does not have to stand as yeast dough does. Breads made this way are called *quick breads*, and include biscuits, muffins, and fruit breads.

■ **LEARN BY DOING**

Why not make your own yeast bread at home? This recipe will make 18 bread rolls. Dissolve a yeast cake in one cup of lukewarm water. Put into a bowl ¼ cup soft butter, 1¼ teaspoons salt, and 2 tablespoons sugar. Add the yeast-and-water mixture to the mixture in the bowl. Mix all these ingredients, and pour in one cup of boiling water. Stir and add one egg. Stir it in until blended, and add 2¾ cups of sifted flour. Mix thoroughly. A soft dough results.

Put the dough in a large bowl that is greased inside. Then turn the dough over so that the upper side is greased. Cover with aluminum foil. Put the bowl in a refrigerator to chill at least two hours, or you can leave it overnight.

When you are ready to bake the rolls, take out the dough and punch it down with your fist. Shape the rolls. Grease muffin tins with shortening or salad oil. Fill the tins to one-third full. Cover the tins with a clean cloth, and allow the rolls to rise in a warm place. Let them rise until doubled in size. Bake them in the oven 15 to 18 minutes at 425°F (220°C). Take them out of the pans at once. ■

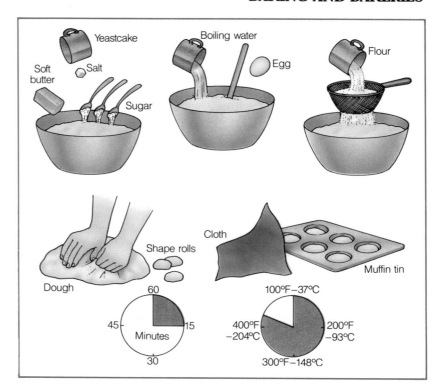

Bread today contains more ingredients than flour, salt, leavening, and water, which were the basic ingredients of ancient bread. Today's bread may contain sweetening, shortening, and sometimes milk. Some commercial bakers *enrich*, or add vitamins and minerals, to bread. Softening substances and chemicals called *preservatives* may be added to make and keep bread soft. Baked foods become stale quickly, if these substances are not added.

Other sweet foods were also made by early bakers. Cakes are mentioned in the Bible, and some have even been found in ancient Egyptian tombs. Today, huge quantities of cakes, pies, cookies, and pastries are made and eaten each year.

Commercial Bakeries Bread baking is not often done in homes today because it is possible to purchase a wide variety of breads from commercial bakeries. Bakeries use three different processes to make bread—the sponge process, the dough process, and the continuous-mix process.

Most large commercial bakeries in the U.S. use the *sponge process*. Ma-

chines do most of the work. To make the sponge, which is the dough, flour is first measured. Then yeast, vitamins, minerals, and water are added to it. The sponge mixture is poured into a huge steel trough. The dough ferments for about 5 hours at 78°F (25.5°C), until it rises. Next the fermented dough is mixed by machine with water, sugar, shortening, butter, eggs, milk, and preservatives. Another machine cuts this mixture into balls, which are rolled flat and kneaded. Then the machine shapes the dough into loaves and puts them into pans. The pans are put into a huge, warm *proof box*, where the loaves rise. After rising, the loaves are baked in very long, tunnel-like ovens at 450°F (232°C) for over 25 minutes. The loaves usually travel on a slow conveyor belt as they bake. After they are finished, they are moved to machines for slicing and wrapping.

Usually only small bakeries use the *dough process* to make bread. The kind of dough that is made is more difficult to move through machinery, so the mixing, shaping, and kneading are usually done by hand. All the

▼ *Bakers produce a variety of tasty cakes and pastries.*

▲ *Balboa, the Spanish explorer, claimed the Pacific Ocean for Spain.*

ingredients are mixed together only one time. The dough ferments for a shorter time—only about three hours—than sponge dough ferments. More yeast is used in this process than in the sponge process. All of the flour ferments, so the bread has a stronger flavor, firmer texture, and harder crust than bread made from sponge dough.

In the *continuous-mix process* a liquid mixture is made that contains part of the flour plus all the other ingredients used to make bread. This mixture is fermented in huge tanks. After fermenting, the mixture is pumped into a continuous-mix machine. The machine blends this mixture with the rest of the flour to make dough. Next the machine pours the same amount of dough into each of thousands of pans to be baked. The bread made by this process is very soft and smooth.

ALSO READ: FERMENTATION, FLOUR MAKING, FOOD PROCESSING, GRAIN, NUTRITION, YEAST.

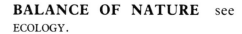

BALANCE OF NATURE see ECOLOGY.

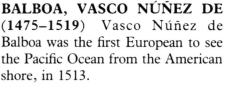

BALBOA, VASCO NÚÑEZ DE (1475–1519) Vasco Núñez de Balboa was the first European to see the Pacific Ocean from the American shore, in 1513.

Balboa was born in Spain but spent about ten years on a Caribbean plantation before helping to start a colony at Darien (now in Panama). Instead of killing the Indians, as did most Spanish *conquistadors* (conquerors), Balboa made some of them his friends. However, he could also be cruel to get what he wanted.

He heard from the Indians about a great sea and a land of gold. He formed an expedition of about 100 Spaniards and 1,000 Indians. For more than three weeks they fought

their way through dense jungle and across deep rivers. At last, Balboa crawled wearily to the top of a high hill and looked out. There he saw the Pacific Ocean, blue and sparkling.

■ **LEARN BY DOING**

Balboa strode into the sea carrying the flag of Spain. He claimed for Spain all the land that this sea touched. Find the Pacific Ocean on a globe or map of the world. Count how many countries that would mean that Spain could own! ■

Balboa did not live to know the size of the "Southern Sea," as he called it. He was beheaded a few years later by a Spanish governor of Darien, known as Pedrarias. Panama's coin, the balboa, is named for him. And when the United States built the Panama Canal, the Pacific entrance city was named Balboa.

ALSO READ: CONQUISTADOR, EXPLORATION, PACIFIC OCEAN, PANAMA.

BALDWIN, JAMES (1924–1987) James Baldwin was an American author best known for his novels and essays about racial conflict in the United States. He was born and raised in the slums of Harlem, in New York City. He went to work in factories after graduating from high school, but he used his evenings for writing. He won a grant in 1948 that enabled him to live and work in Europe. His first book, *Go tell It on the Mountain*, was published in 1953 and was an instant success. It is the story of a 14-year-old black boy growing up in Harlem. It was followed by a group of essays, *Notes of a Native Son* (1955).

Baldwin returned to the U.S. in 1957 and became active in the civil rights movement. He also continued to turn out best-selling books such as *Nobody Knows My Name* (essays) and *Another Country* (a novel). One of his outstanding collections of essays, *The*

▼ *U.S. novelist James Baldwin wrote about what it means to be black in America.*

Fire Next Time, criticizes American society for the way it treats black citizens. In 1965, Baldwin wrote the play *Blues for Mr. Charlie* that was performed on Broadway.

ALSO READ: CIVIL RIGHTS MOVEMENT.

BALL The first toy balls were probably rounded stones, which were rolled or tossed. Thousands of years ago, balls were used as weapons. They were thrown at enemies and game animals.

Balls are rolled, tossed, and hit in many games. Baseball, basketball, tennis, bowling, volleyball, billiards, golf, and many other games use balls of some kind. We usually think of a ball as perfectly *spherical*, or round. This is not always so. A football, for example, is oval instead of round.

Balls can be made of almost any material, including snow. The Aztec and Mayan Indians played an old game like basketball with a rubber ball. North American Indians played lacrosse and other games with balls made of animal hides. Animal skins still provide the covering of some kinds of balls. Cowhide is the outer surface of most baseballs. Plastics are now widely used in making different kinds of balls. Others are made of solid wood, rubber, cork, animal hair, and string.

There are many sizes and weights of balls. Maybe you have seen a big, heavy, sand-filled "medicine" ball in a gym. Compare that with a light-weight table tennis ball. One of the smallest balls is the kind used in a game of jacks. It must be tiny enough to fit in a child's hand. It must also be bouncy enough to give the player time to pick up the jacks. Today, balls for each sport have a standard shape, size, and weight.

ALSO READ: SPORTS.

BALLAD see FOLK SONG.

BALLET Many people think that ballet dancing is one of the most beautiful arts. Steps and movement are put together with music, costume, and scenery to entertain an audience. Some parts of a ballet are danced by a group, others by one or two main dancers. The ballet often tells a story, but it does not have to.

Learning the Steps Both boys and girls study ballet and learn the same steps. It may take as long as ten years to learn to control the body and do the steps. Dancers must also learn a language of gesture, of *pantomime*.

There are five basic positions of the feet that a dancer must learn. All the dance movements begin and end in one of these positions. There are six main movements: bending, stretching, raising, sliding, darting, and turning. They have French names because the movements were devel-

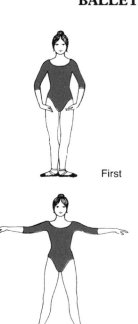
First

Second

Third

Fourth

Fifth

▲ *The five basic feet positions of classical ballet.*

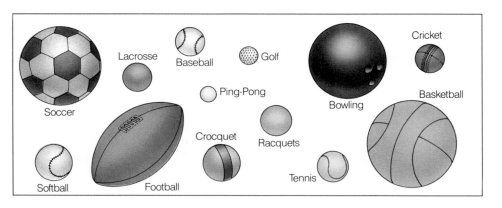

Soccer
Lacrosse
Baseball
Golf
Ping-Pong
Cricket
Bowling
Basketball
Crocquet
Racquets
Softball
Football
Tennis

▼ *Two ballet dancers in performance. To reach the top in this demanding profession takes years of hard work and determination.*

oped in France. Ballet dancers, in whatever country they live, use these French names.

A girl dancer must learn the very difficult art of dancing on her toes, or *sur les pointes*. Ballet shoes have a hard block at the toes, on which the dancers stand. Dancers even darn the toes of the shoes so that the extra roughness guards against slipping.

Boys learn a variety of different jumps and leaps. All begin and end in one of the five basic foot positions. There are many small jumps. But the *grand jeté* is a long leap through the air. The *entrechat* is a jump straight up, with the feet changing position very rapidly in the air. The feet seem to be "twinkling," when they change position as many as eight times before the dancer lands.

Not only students must practice. The most famous ballet dancers spend long hours each day practicing their moves and keeping their bodies in good condition.

Story of the Ballet A lavish entertainment was put on to celebrate a wedding in the royal French court at Versailles, in 1581. For the first time, dance and music were combined to act out a story. This *ballet de cour* (court ballet) was the beginning of the art of ballet. Opera was developing at the same time. Both as dance and as part of opera, ballet became popular. King Louis XIV of France sometimes performed in ballets. He so loved the art that he started the Royal Academy of Dance in 1661.

Ballet developed over the next 200 years and spread to other European countries. The major steps and movements which are still used were established, and the special hard-toed shoe for toe dancing was invented. Audiences especially liked the romantic love story ballets, such as *Giselle* and *La Sylphide*.

The czars (kings) of Russia enjoyed ballet. Russian composers wrote music especially for the dance. Peter Tchaikovsky, one of the first major composers of ballet music, wrote *Swan Lake*, *Sleeping Beauty*, and *Nutcracker*. These ballets are still widely performed. Children especially enjoy seeing *Nutcracker*, a Christmas story, during the holiday season.

Modern Ballet A young Russian, Sergei Diaghilev of the Ballet Russe, was interested in modern art and music in the early 20th century. He felt that great ballet was more than just great dancing. He turned to such young composers as Igor Stravinsky and Maurice Ravel for new music. Famous artists, such as Pablo Picasso, made costumes and scenery designs for the Ballet Russe. Diaghilev incorporated the informal modern dance into the formal classical ballet, giving new ballets of freshness and excitement.

In 1909, Diaghilev took the Ballet Russe to Paris. The performances were a sensation. The great Russian dancer, Anna Pavlova, performed with them. One of the young male dancers was Vaslav Nijinsky. His amazing skill and grace were such that he is remembered as one of the great dancers of all time. His bright career was cut sadly short by insanity.

The Ballet Russe started the age of modern ballet. The Sadler's Wells Ballet, later called the Royal Ballet, was formed in England in the 1930's. One of its great dancers, Dame Margot Fonteyn, often danced with Rudolf Nureyev, a Soviet dancer who sought refuge in the West in 1961. The U.S.S.R. trains many fine dancers, who perform with leading com-

▼ *Dancers of the Ballet Folklorico de Mexico perform* Los Mayas, *a ballet by Amalia Hernandez.*

panies such as the Bolshoi Ballet. Many other countries have national ballet companies that perform colorful ballets based on their nation's folk tales, besides the well-known classical and modern ballets.

There have been several important American ballet companies. One is the New York City Ballet. Its choreographer, George Balanchine, created many beautiful classical and modern ballets. American Ballet Theater is another leading U.S. company. Others include Dance Theater of Harlem and Ballet West. Ballet has found its way into musical comedy, beginning with *On Your Toes* in 1935. Agnes de Mille created truly American ballets, such as *Rodeo* and *Fall River Legend*. Many ballets now combine American jazz and rock music with classical movements, bringing ballet to a wider audience.

ALSO READ: DANCE; DUNCAN, ISADORA; FONTEYN, MARGOT; MODERN DANCE; NIJINSKY, VASLAV; PAVLOVA, ANNA; TCHAIKOVSKY, PETER.

BALLOON Have you ever blown up a toy balloon and watched it float in the air? It probably came down almost at once, because it was heavier than air. But if you could have heated the air in the balloon, it might have risen to the ceiling. Hot air weighs less than normal, or "cold" air, so the balloon would have floated up.

Two French brothers, Joseph and Jacques Montgolfier, and their sister Marianne, who lived in France during the 18th century, watched smoke and small bits of ash rise up the chimney of a fireplace. They realized that hot air is lighter than cold air. Joseph borrowed some silk cloth from his landlady and made a big bag with a hole in one end. He held the hole over a fire. The bag swelled up and floated to the ceiling. Joseph had invented the *hot-air balloon*.

Joseph, Jacques, and Marianne

The first ballet performed in America was in New York in 1827. The audience, shocked at how little clothing the dancers wore, walked out.

▼ *The first manned flight of a hot-air balloon took place in Paris, France. The date was November 21, 1783.*

▲ *The first hydrogen balloon rose above Paris on December 1, 1783.*

▼ *Weather balloons provide information about winds and weather. They carry scientific instruments high into the sky.*

to fill balloons with *hydrogen*. Hydrogen is a gas even lighter than hot air, so his balloons could fly longer and higher. Professor Charles's first manned balloon flight was on December 1, 1783.

Hydrogen is dangerous because just a small spark makes an air-hydrogen mixture explode. But it was used in balloons and airships until *helium* was discovered many years later. Helium is also a lighter-than-air gas, and it does not explode.

Ballooning quickly became very popular all over the world. Many contests were held to see whose balloon could go fastest, highest, or farthest. Armies used balloons in wars. They were usually tied to the ground and flown like kites. The man on board was high in the air, so he could see what the enemy was doing and tell his army. *Observation* balloons like this were used by both the Union and Confederate forces during the Civil War. Moored balloons were used for defense against low-flying bombing planes in World War II.

Experience gained with balloons helped aviators to build large, steerable *airships*. But balloons were still useful. Huge, unmanned plastic balloons now collect weather information. They carry scientific instruments that relay measurements to the ground by radio. They fly as high as 50,000 feet (15,000 m) and can go around the world many times before they wear out. They measure the winds, temperature, pressure, and humidity.

The first space balloon, Echo I, was inflated in space at a height of more than 1,000 miles (1,609 km) above the Earth by NASA in 1960. It was used to locate and track communication satellites.

Sport ballooning has become a hobby, particularly in the United States. Hot-air balloons have burners fed by bottled gas to heat the air. A pilot turns on the burner to heat the air and make the balloon rise higher.

then made a linen balloon, more than 100 feet (30 m) around. They lined it with paper, so the air would not leak out. They built a big fire in the marketplace at Annonay, France, on June 5, 1783. They filled the balloon with hot air. The crowd was amazed that eight men had to hold the balloon down. When the men let go, it rose over 950 feet (300 m) high, and after the air cooled it came down gently more than one mile (1.6 km) away. Jacques soon built another large balloon. It had a basket underneath for a fire so the air would stay hot inside the bag. Under the basket was a cage for a duck, a rooster, and a sheep. The King and Queen of France watched as the balloon took off in front of the Royal Palace, on September 19, 1783. It flew for eight minutes and traveled a mile and a half (2.4 km).

The brothers sent up another balloon on November 21, 1783. The balloon carried two people, Jean-François Pilatre de Rozier and the Marquis of Arlandes. They flew 5 miles (8 km) in 25 minutes. They were the first true aviators.

At about the same time J. A. C. Charles, also French, discovered how

▲ *Sports ballooning is a popular modern pastime. Enthusiasts enjoy the fun of silent, floating flight.*

Balloonists have flown the Atlantic and Pacific oceans, and reached a height of 101,520 feet (30,942 m) above the ground.

■ LEARN BY DOING

Would you like to find out how far balloons can travel? You can do an experiment that will give you some idea. First you need some helium balloons, maybe from an amusement park or carnival. Buy some postcards at the post office. Address the cards to yourself, and add a message asking the finder to write on the card when and where it was found and to mail it back to you. Punch holes in the cards, tie one to each balloon, and release the balloons. Some of the balloons may be lost, but you will get some interesting replies.

Find out the wind speed and direction at the time you released the balloons, by checking the weather bureau or from the next day's newspaper. Mark the answers you get on a map to see where your balloons traveled. What would have happened if the wind had been from another direction? ■

ALSO READ: AIR, AIRSHIP, AVIATION.

BALTIC SEA Ships can sail from the Atlantic Ocean deep into northern Europe by way of the Baltic Sea. The Baltic Sea is 930 miles (1,496 km) long and 400 miles (643 km) across at its widest part. The sea is fairly shallow, averaging about 300 feet (91 m) deep. (See the map with the article on EUROPE.)

A ship must navigate a narrow channel off the Danish coast to get to the Baltic from the North Sea. The ship can then travel as far east as Leningrad in the Soviet Union, or as far north as Kemi in Finland. It can stop along the way in Denmark, Sweden, West Germany, East Germany, Poland, and the three Baltic republics of the Soviet Union—Estonia, Latvia, and Lithuania. The busy ports of Copenhagen (Denmark); Stockholm (Sweden), and Gdansk (Poland) are on Baltic shores.

The Kiel Canal is a shortcut from the Baltic to the North Sea, across the narrow neck of West Germany. Other canals join the Baltic with the Arctic Ocean and the Volga River.

ALSO READ: DENMARK, NORTH SEA.

BANDS see ORCHESTRAS AND BANDS.

BANGLADESH This Asian nation came into being in 1971. Before then it was called East Pakistan and was one of the two widely separate regions making up the Muslim country of Pakistan. East Pakistan was the poorer of the two. Its Bengali people demanded greater self-government and aid for their region from the richer West Pakistan. This protest led to rebellion, and West Pakistan sent troops to restore order. But the Indian army helped the Bengalis, who defeated the West Pakistanis and won their independence in 1971. Bangladesh ("Bengal nation") was born.

In 1978, three Americans, Ben Abruzzo, Max Anderson, and Larry Newman, became the first balloonists to cross the Atlantic Ocean. Their balloon, the *Double Eagle II*, soared from Presque Isle, Maine, to a field near Paris, France.

▼ *In Bangladesh most people live by farming. Here people plant rice seedlings in a paddy field.*

BANGLADESH

Capital City: Dacca (3,459,000 people).
Area: 55,598 square miles (143,999 sq. km).
Population: 112,760,000.
Government: Republic.
Natural Resources: Farmland, fish.
Export Products: Jute, leather, tea, fish, hides and skins.
Unit of Money: Taka.
Official Language: Bengali. (English is also spoken.)

Deep-rooted poverty has continually troubled the country, one of the world's ten most densely populated. Bangladesh has few natural resources, other than its land and water. Poor food production and serious overcrowding have led to periods of famine. The country has a constitution that provides for a democratic presidential form of government, but martial law (law administered by military forces) was imposed in 1982.

Bangladesh, on the Bay of Bengal, is about the size of Wisconsin. The biggest cities are the capital, Dacca, and the main port, Chittagong. The climate is hot and humid. In the rainy season, branches of the Ganges and Brahmaputra rivers flood the flat land. Cyclones and tidal waves coming from the bay often inflict damage in the delta region. Almost all of the people live in small farming villages. Many animals live in the forests, including tigers, elephants, and water buffaloes. Rice, jute (used to make twine and sacks), tea, and sugarcane are the main crops. Freshwater and saltwater fishing are also important, and hides are exported.

ALSO READ: GANGES RIVER, INDIA, PAKISTAN.

If one dollar had been banked 200 years ago and left to accumulate at 10 percent per annum interest, it would now be worth $150 million.

BANKS AND BANKING Today, we take banks for granted. But before there were any banks, people had to carry money with them if they went on a journey. Imagine you lived in England, centuries ago. You have to travel from London to Plymouth. You do not want to carry many gold coins because there are robbers along the way. So you give your gold coins to a London goldsmith to hold. Goldsmiths always kept their gold and jewels in safe places.

The goldsmith gives you a *receipt*, showing that the goldsmith accepted

▶ *Early Italian bankers traded from stalls or benches in the street. From the Italian* banca *("bench") comes our word bank.*

responsibility for the coins. The goldsmith will return the coins when you come back to London and return the receipt. For this service, you pay a small sum to the goldsmith.

When you reach Plymouth, you need money to buy new clothes. You borrow ten gold coins from a friendly merchant who is going to London. In exchange, you give the merchant a note telling the goldsmith in London to give ten of your gold coins to the merchant. The goldsmith has served as a banker.

Hundreds of years before Christ, people in Greece and Egypt loaned money to other people. Later, the Romans made laws to control money-lending. But there were no banks such as those we have today.

The first real bank was probably the Bank of San Giorgio in Genoa, Italy. It began in 1148. Other banks soon opened in other countries. The first bank in the United States was the Bank of North America, in Philadelphia, in 1782. It was a great success. There were two other private American banks in 1784, one in New York and one in Boston. In 1791, Congress issued a charter, or permit, for the First Bank of the United States. This bank was in Philadelphia and lasted until 1811, when Congress refused to renew the bank's permit. Hundreds of new banks were then given permits by state governments. The Federal Government set up the *National Banking System* and also issued the first Federal paper money in 1862.

Borrowing, Saving, and Paying A bank is a kind of store that deals in money. You can borrow money from banks to buy homes, automobiles, or other goods. Towns and cities borrow from banks to build schools and roads. Banks lend money to makers of airplanes, cars, clothing, and other things. In this way manufacturers can buy supplies, new machines, or put up new buildings. Without banks, factories would close, and mil-

▲ *The Bank of England, founded in 1694, served as a model for many later banks.*

lions of people could not pay for goods.

If you borrow money from a bank, you must pay it back with *interest*. That is, you pay the bank a little more than you borrow. When you *deposit*, or put, money in a *savings account* in a bank, the bank pays you interest. It then uses your money to make loans to others. The interest the bank charges for lending money is higher than the interest it pays to depositors, so the bank makes a profit by making loans. Money in a savings account cannot always be taken out, or *withdrawn*, any time the depositor wishes. For some types of accounts, the bank wants advanced warning about any withdrawals.

Some banks pay no interest on *checking accounts* because the money in these accounts may not stay in the bank, as savings do. The depositor may write *checks*. A check is a written order telling the bank to pay a certain amount of money to a certain person or company. People with checking accounts do not have to carry large amounts of cash.

Besides lending money, banks also give advice to customers about using their money in helpful ways. For example, people may pay a bank to take care of their money when they die.

There was not a single bank in all America before the Revolution. People just borrowed money from each other.

▲ *Bank strong rooms guard money and valuables. The strong rooms are protected by massive doors, electronic alarms and other anti-theft devices.*

▼ *Sir Frederick Banting, Canadian medical scientist.*

They arrange to put their money and other property "in trust." They tell the bank how the money is to be used. When they die, the bank's *trust department* will see that the money is used as they wished.

There are many kinds of banks. *Commercial* banks, which include state and national banks, make loans and investments. *Savings* banks accept time deposits (mutual savings are owned by the depositors). *Central* banks hold the cash reserves of a country. The central banking system of the United States is the Federal Reserve System. It consists of 12 Federal Reserve Banks that make loans to regular state and national banks. They regulate the money of the U.S. government.

All banks must obey special state or federal banking laws. All are visited by bank examiners, who make sure that the banks are run properly and are sticking to the laws.

ALSO READ: ECONOMICS, MONEY, SAVINGS.

BANNEKER, BENJAMIN (1731–1806) One of the best-known blacks in early U.S. history was the mathematician Benjamin Banneker.

Banneker was born a free man in Maryland at a time when most blacks were slaves. His grandmother taught him to read the Bible by the time he was four. Banneker attended a Quaker school. George Ellicott, a friend, got him interested in astronomy. Banneker charted the movement of the stars so accurately that he published his own almanac from 1792 until he died.

President George Washington appointed him assistant planner and surveyor for the new capital city. The chief architect was Pierre Charles L'Enfant, a Frenchman. As a surveyor, Banneker was allowed to see L'Enfant's drawings, which the architect usually kept secret. L'Enfant resigned and Banneker's friend, George Ellicott, replaced him as chief architect. The angry L'Enfant took all his drawings with him. But Banneker was able to reconstruct the plan from memory. The streets of Washington, D.C., still reflect Banneker's effort.

ALSO READ: DISTRICT OF COLUMBIA.

BANTING, SIR FREDERICK (1891–1941) The disease called *diabetes* used to cause many deaths. But today, people suffering from diabetes can be treated with the hormone *insulin*. The discoverer of insulin was Frederick Banting, a Canadian surgeon.

Besides being a surgeon, Banting worked as an instructor in medicine at the University of Toronto. One evening, while preparing a lecture on a body organ called the *pancreas*, he read an article on the problem of diabetes. Doctors knew that certain glands in the pancreas produce a hormone that helps the body make use of sugar, and that a person would get diabetes if these glands failed to make enough of the hormone. But no one had been able to extract the pancreas hormone for use as a medicine.

Banting began work on the problem under the direction of Professor John Macleod. Late in 1921, he succeeded, with the help of two assistants, Charles Best and James Collip. The hormone, later called insulin, was tested first on a dog and then on a child dying of diabetes. It worked. Banting and Macleod won the 1923 Nobel Prize in physiology and medicine for their work. Banting shared his award with Best, and Macleod shared his with Collip.

ALSO READ: HORMONE, HUMAN BODY, MEDICINE.

BARBADOS   see WEST INDIES.

BARBARY COAST   The northern Africa coastal region, from Libya to Morocco, was once called the Barbary Coast. The name comes from the *Berber* tribes, which still live there. The Barbary Coast area was populated by family tribes, headed by chiefs called *sheiks*. These sheikdoms traded with regions to the south. Many sheiks also financed pirates who sailed the Mediterranean Sea. These pirates captured ships and often sold foreign crew members as slaves.

The United States paid the sheiks a large sum of money each year, starting in 1795, to keep the Barbary pirates from attacking U.S. ships. The sheiks demanded more money in 1801. When the United States refused to pay more, the sheiks declared war. They captured the U.S. ship *Philadelphia*. Lieutenant Stephen Decatur of the U.S. Navy and 84 Navy volunteers sailed into the harbor of Tripoli, the pirates' main city, on February 16, 1804. The Americans burned the *Philadelphia*. The next year the U.S. Marines attacked the pirates' lair at Derna, and the war soon came to an end. After the war with these Barbary Coast pirates, the U.S. government realized that a strong, regular navy would be needed.

ALSO READ: ALGERIA, LIBYA, MOROCCO, NAVY, PIRATES AND PRIVATEERS, TUNISIA.

BAR CODE   When you buy something at a store, have you ever noticed a pattern of black and white stripes on the carton or package? It's called a bar code, and it helps the people who run and own the store.

The stripes make a number in a code known as binary code. In this code, a thick stripe stands for 1 and a thin stripe for 0. Each product that you buy has a different number. At the store's check-out, a machine "reads" the bar code and converts it into a signal that goes to the store's computer. The computer looks up the price of each item and prepares the sales check. In addition, it works out how many products are sold every day. It can then order new supplies.

When you go shopping, look to see how many different goods are marked with bar codes.

ALSO READ: BINARY SYSTEM, COMPUTER.

Piracy along the North African Barbary coast was a recognized profession from earliest times. It was only finally stamped out by the French conquest of Algiers in 1830.

A bar code contains a digital message turned into bars that can be decoded by a light pen. This code records the number assigned to a book by its publisher.

▲ *A battle in the harbor of Tripoli on the Barbary Coast. Two famous American sailors fought for their lives. Reuben James stepped in to save Stephen Decatur from being killed.*

Some trees, including the Mediterranean cork oak, produce very thick bark. This is stripped from the tree at intervals and is the source of commercial cork.

BARDEEN, JOHN (born 1908)

John Bardeen is an American scientist who is best known for his work in finding out about how different kinds of solids carry electric currents. This is very important because his work made possible the invention of the *transistor*. The transistor is one of the most important inventions of the 20th century. It made possible the modern computer, for one thing.

With William Shockley and Walter Brattain, Bardeen was awarded the 1956 Nobel Prize in physics for his work on the transistor.

Transistors are tiny electronic devices that can amplify electric currents—make them stronger. Today's radio and TV sets and computers can contain hundreds or even thousands of transistors. It is now possible to put thousands of transistors on a tiny piece of silicon. We know this as the "silicon chip."

In 1972, John Bardeen won a second Nobel Prize, with Leon Cooper and John Schrieffer, for his work on *superconductivity*—the vanishing of electrical resistance in some metals when they are cooled to very low temperatures.

ALSO READ: CRYOGENICS, SEMICONDUCTOR, TRANSISTOR.

▲ *Cork bark of a pine tree showing the deep grooves caused by the splitting of the bark as the tree grows.*

BARK The "skin" of a tree is called bark. If you know something about bark, you can tell what *species*, or type, a tree is, even in winter when the leaves are gone. Many animals, such as deer and beaver, eat the bark of some trees.

Some trees have light-colored bark. Trembling aspens and some birches are covered with white or light gray bark. The bark on other trees is black or dark brown. A young tree often has bark of a different color from the bark on an old tree of the same type. Some trees have very thin bark. On others, such as the huge Douglas fir, the bark may be more than 12 inches (30 cm) thick.

When you look at a young tree stem, the part you see is a thin protective layer called the *epidermis*. This is soon replaced by *cork*, special tissue made of dead cells whose walls contain waterproof substances. The cork protects the stem from injury, disease, and water loss. The cork splits as the diameter of the stem increases, causing the grooved or peeling appearance of many kinds of bark. The second layer of bark, inside the cork, is the *cork cambium*. This layer is

▼ *Bark is made up of non-living, waterproof cells. Beneath the bark is the vascular cambium, which produces the phloem and xylem cells on which the tree depends for growth. Each ring in a tree stump represents a year's growth of xylem cells. So, by counting the rings, you can find how old the tree is. Phloem cells are soft, and each year's growth becomes part of the bark covering, which thickens as the tree grows.*

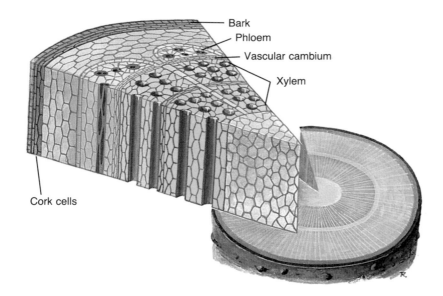

Bark
Phloem
Vascular cambium
Xylem
Cork cells

made up of living cells that add new cork as the stem grows. The cork and cork cambium together are often called the *outer bark.*

Just inside the cork cambium are the two layers of the *inner* bark. The first of these is the *cortex.* The cortex of young stems contains chlorophyll and manufactures food. But this activity stops when the cork forms, and the cortex is then used to store the food produced in the leaves. The innermost layer of bark is the *phloem,* composed of thin-walled tubes that carry food dissolved in water. The tubes are strengthened by tough fibers called *bast.*

Never pull the bark off a tree, because the growing layer will be damaged. Some trees, however, are grown just for the substances obtained by cutting, or "lapping," their bark. *Resins,* sticky substances from pines, are used in turpentine and other products. Rubber is the white, juicy *latex* of the rubber tree.

■ LEARN BY DOING

You can "collect" bark without hurting trees, if you collect bark *tracings.* Place a sheet of paper against the bark of a tree and rub firmly with charcoal or black crayon. Collect as many kinds of samples as you can. Is some bark smooth? Is some rough? What patterns do you see? ■

ALSO READ: PLANT, TREE.

Practice recognizing a tree from its bark. Here are four examples:

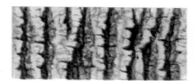

Ridged bark, such as oak

Banded bark, such as cherry

Stringy bark, such as redwood

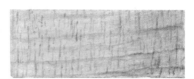

Smooth bark, such as beech

BARLEY see GRAIN.

BARNUM, P. T. (1810–1891) Phineas Taylor Barnum was often called "the world's greatest showman." He as also a pioneer of modern advertising because he used publicity of every kind to draw people to his circus.

Barnum was born in Bethel, Connecticut. He did not have much schooling, but he was smart and clever at fooling people. He also discovered that many people liked to be fooled.

In his first show he exhibited a midget, known as "General Tom Thumb." Other famous attractions promoted by Barnum included Jenny Lind, a singer called the "Swedish Nightingale," and Jumbo, a huge African elephant. Barnum put together his first circus in 1871. His main rival, James A. Bailey, later became his partner. Together, they started the Barnum and Bailey Circus, also called "the Greatest Show on Earth." Ringling Brothers bought out the show in the early 1900's.

To advertise his shows, Barnum sent "advance men" ahead of the circus to cover a town with brightly

▼ *Phineas T. Barnum, great American showman, developed a sensational method of advertising called "ballyhoo" to promote his famous traveling circus.*

Air pressure decreases the higher you go. So airplane pilots use instruments called *altimeters* to show the height at which they are flying. One kind of altimeter works just like an aneroid barometer. The higher the airplane flies, the lower the outside pressure becomes. The altimeter reading shows the height.

colored posters. Then brass bands and a parade left no one in doubt that the circus had come to town. Above all, he used spectacular words and phrases to describe the wonders of his circus. Barnum was a show-off even in his private life. Whenever a train passed by his home, he would have an elephant out plowing in a nearby field as if to show passengers where the world's greatest showman lived.

ALSO READ: CIRCUS.

BAROMETER The barometer is an instrument that measures air pressure and is useful in forecasting the weather. The first barometer was built in 1643 by Evangelista Torricelli, an Italian scientist. He filled a long glass tube, closed at one end, with mercury. He turned the tube upside-down in a bowl of mercury. Air, pressing down on the mercury in the bowl, held the mercury up in the tube.

A newer type is the *aneroid* ("without air") barometer. It is round, has a glass cover, and looks like a wall clock. It has a dial and a hand that moves to indicate the air pressure.

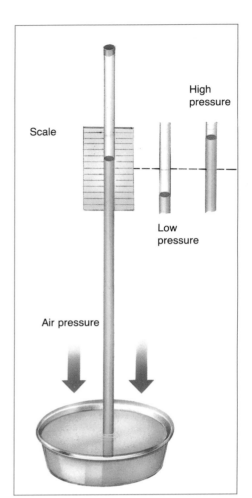

Scale

High pressure

Low pressure

Air pressure

Partly empty vacuum can

▶ *An aneroid barometer shows changes in air pressure when the metal vacuum can expands or contracts. The bending of the sides of the can moves the hands on the dial, so you can read the pressure.*

Behind the dial is a small metal can with thin walls. Most of the air has been removed from the can. The sides of the can bend in from the air pressure. The greater the pressure, the more the can bends. The bending moves the hand on the dial to give a reading of the pressure.

■ **LEARN BY DOING**

You can make a barometer to show changes in air pressure. Use a long piece of clear plastic tubing. Suck water part of the way up it from a dish. Stop up the top with a piece of plasticine. Fix the tube to an upright. Place a scale where the water level is. As the air pressure rises and falls, so the water level will rise and fall. What happens just before a storm? ■

ALSO READ: AIR, AIR PRESSURE, WEATHER.

BAROQUE PERIOD (1600–1750)

Bursting with life. That might describe Baroque—a period in the arts when much artistic activity was springing to life. In music, we think of Baroque as lively, with different melodic lines going on at the same time, and musicians ornamenting notes and trills. The music of George Frederick Handel (1685–1759) is from the period of Baroque. At this time new musical instruments were being designed and the arts of the opera were being developed.

In art, what is called *high Baroque* took place in Italy between 1630 and 1680. The great religious zeal of a time called the *Counter Reformation* was being expressed in big, color-filled paintings showing strong feelings. Baroque artists often combined three arts—architecture, painting, and sculpture. The master of three

▼ *Bernini's statue of* St. Teresa *(1644) in a church in Rome. Bernini has been called the creator of the Baroque style in art.*

▲ *Ceiling fresco (painting on plaster) by Giambattista Tiepolo, in the Residenz Palace, Würzburg, West Germany.*

arts as one was Giovanni Bernini (1598–1680). He worked for years to help finish the Basilica of Saint Peter in Rome. He combined architecture, painting, and sculpture in one unified form of art.

Another great master of painting was the Venetian, Giambattista Tiepolo (1696–1770), who painted the ceiling in Germany (see picture). You seem to be looking up through a hole in the ceiling at a sky full of architecture, flying figures, and clouds. To make the scene look real, legs seem to overhang the rim of the ceiling, and the clouds seem to be drifting into the room where you stand. Tiepolo wants to convince you that the scene is going on as you watch it, and that you may become part of it. This is very Baroque.

The great artist Peter Paul Rubens (1577–1640) studied in Italy for eight years as Baroque was beginning. He then went back to his home in Antwerp (now in Belgium) and made it a center of European art. His *Triumph of Love* is full of energy and golden light. The picture seems to be beyond the limits of the frame, in true Baroque open style.

The architecture of the Baroque period was also full of life. Elements of classical architecture appear, but in a distorted and fantastically decorated form, often creating rich surfaces that

▼ *Bernini's* baldachino *(1624-1633) towers above the high altar of Saint Peter's Basilica in Rome. It is typically Baroque in its energy and decoration.*

▲ The Triumph of Love *by Peter Paul Rubens is another Baroque masterpiece.*

catch the sunlight and create interesting shadows. Such exuberance is very Baroque.

Baroque in Italy was a grand style. It appealed to royalty throughout Europe, and they copied it in building palaces. In France, Baroque is called the style of Louis XIV. He was king from 1643 to 1715. In 1661 he began a great monument to himself, the Palace of Versailles. Its Hall of Mirrors, its Trianon and other elaborate features, fancy, ornate, and covered with *gilt* (gold paint) decoration, speak of a golden period of splendor and spirit.

Look around your city for an example of the Baroque style. Architects have tried to imitate Baroque in auditoriums, theaters, state capitols, and hotel lobbies. They try to give visitors a feeling of elegance. Look for gold decorations, high, domed ceilings, fancy mirrors, statues of cherubs, and large, showy wall pieces. That is Louis XIV style or Baroque. The U.S. Capitol dome is an example of Baroque influence in the United States.

ALSO READ: ARCHITECTURE, ART HISTORY, BACH FAMILY, CATHEDRAL, PROTESTANT REFORMATION, VERSAILLES.

▼ *Sir James Barrie, Scottish novelist and playwright.*

BARRIE, JAMES M. (1860–1937) Sir James Matthew Barrie wrote many plays and books. Barrie was born in Kirriemuir, Scotland. His father was a weaver. From the time he was a little boy he wanted to write. Barrie had no children of his own. But he loved the child's world of make-believe and never forgot what fun it is to be very young.

His most famous play is *Peter Pan*, first produced in 1904. *Peter Pan* is the story of a little boy who doesn't want to grow up. He lives in Never-Never Land with Indians, lost boys, pirates, and the fairy Tinker Bell. A little girl named Wendy Darling and her two brothers share Peter's adventures with Captain Hook, a nasty-tempered pirate with a hook for a hand. Barrie gave all the profits from *Peter Pan* to a London children's hospital.

The Little Minister, a novel that Barrie later made into a play, was his first success. Two of Barrie's other well-known plays are *The Admirable Crichton* and *Dear Brutus*.

ALSO READ: CHILDREN'S LITERATURE.

BARRYMORE FAMILY The Barrymores were one of the most famous families of actors in American theater. The family's theatrical history began with Maurice Barrymore (1847–1905). He was born Herbert Blythe, in India, and changed his name when he grew up. He married an American actress named Georgiana Drew. Her parents and her brother, John Drew, were also actors. Georgiana and Maurice had three children who became actors.

Lionel Barrymore (1878–1954) was the oldest. Born in Philadelphia, he first acted on the stage in 1893. He became one of the first stage actors to succeed in movies. He starred in the "Dr. Kildare" movie series, and each year on radio portrayed "Scrooge" in

▲ *Ethel Barrymore, in a scene from* The Corn is Green.

Dicken's *A Christmas Carol.* He wrote a book about his family called *We Barrymores.*

Ethel Barrymore (1879–1959) was educated in a convent and went on to become the "first lady" of the American theater. Her first stage success was in *Captain Jinks of the Horse Marines* in 1900. She acted in *Camille, The Corn Is Green,* and many other plays, as well as in movies, including *None but the Lonely Heart* for which she won an Academy Award in 1944. She wrote an autobiography called *Memories.*

John Barrymore (1882–1942) was the youngest of the three. His stage career brought him worldwide fame, especially in the role of Hamlet in Shakespeare's play. He turned to movies and made many classics, such as *Grand Hotel* (1932). One of the most romantic actors of his day, he was called "The Great Profile" because a side view of his face was so handsome. *Good Night, Sweet Prince,*

written by Gene Fowler, tells the fascinating and tragic story of his life. John Barrymore's daughter Diana (1921–1960) also became an actress.

ALSO READ: ACTORS AND ACTING, MOTION PICTURES.

BARTON, CLARA (1821–1912) Clara Barton, the founder of the American Red Cross, was born on a farm in Oxford, Massachusetts. After 18 years of teaching, she was the first woman hired to work as a clerk in the United States Patent Office in Washington, D.C. Miss Barton worked there during the Civil War. She traveled to battlefields in Virginia and Maryland to help the wounded soldiers, who were not getting proper care. Distressed at the conditions she saw, she sought donations of food and delivered meals to the wounded men herself, along with medical supplies. Although not a nurse, she helped bandage the soldiers' wounds. Soldiers called her the "Angel of the Battlefields."

Many badly wounded soldiers could not get in touch with their families when the Civil War ended. Clara formed an organization to trace missing people. She soon had files on more than 20,000 people. She worked so hard she became ill, so she went to Europe to rest.

War broke out between France and Prussia (now Germany) in 1870 while Miss Barton was in Europe. Again she nursed the wounded. She also learned about the International Red Cross, newly founded to help wounded soldiers, prisoners of war, and their families. She returned to the United States in 1881, founded the American Red Cross, and served as its first president. Today, the Red Cross is known for the help it provides in disasters such as earthquakes, hurricanes, or floods.

ALSO READ: RED CROSS.

▲ *John Barrymore, "The Great Profile."*

▼ *Clara Barton, the soldiers' friend.*

▲ *A young baseball player up at bat. Many baseball stars learn to play in Little League games.*

▼ *Baseball attracts big crowds of spectators, and many more fans enjoy the big games on TV.*

BASEBALL One of the most popular sports in the United States is baseball. The game began in the eastern United States in the mid 1880's. It quickly spread throughout the country and became the "national pastime." Today, baseball is very popular in Puerto Rico, Cuba, Japan, Taiwan, Canada, some Latin American countries, and parts of Europe.

In the spring and summer, Americans of all ages play on organized baseball teams. There are high school and college teams; there is *Little League, American Legion, Babe Ruth*, and amateur adult league baseball.

A *league* is a group of baseball teams that play each other many times during the season. The two major leagues in the U.S. are the American League and the National League. The teams in these two leagues are made up of some of the world's best baseball players, called *professionals*. The *World Series* is the high point of the professional baseball season. It is really not a *world* series, but a series of games between the best team from each U.S. league. The winner must win four out of seven games to become the champion team.

How Baseball Began People played games with balls and sticks hundreds of years ago. But their games were not well organized. People in one town played the game one way, while players in other places used different rules. In 1845, Alexander Cartwright drew the first baseball *diamond*. The first game between two organized teams took place the next year in New Jersey. Some people claim that Abner Doubleday drew up the rules for modern baseball, and that the game was first played in Cooperstown, New York. There is no real proof for this claim. But the Baseball Hall of Fame is now located in Cooperstown.

How to Play A professional baseball field is called a *diamond*, but it is not diamond-shaped. It is really a square 90 feet (27.4 m) on each side. At each corner of the square is a *base*. The bases are called *first*, *second*, *third*, and *home*. The first three bases are marked by bags. The bags are square in shape and are stuffed canvas. Instead of a bag at home base, there is a flat plate, called *home plate*. The area inside the bases is the *infield*. The area beyond the bases is the *outfield*.

There are nine baseball players on a

COMMON TERMS IN BASEBALL

Ball
A pitch that is outside the strike zone.

Batting average
The number of hits a player makes divided by the times he has batted.

Double header
Two games for the price of one. The games follow one another. It is sometimes called a "bargain bill."

Double play
Putting out two players at the same time.

Error
A mistake by a player that allows a runner to be safe when he should have been put out.

Fielder's choice
A fielder's decision to put out a runner instead of a batter.

Foul ball
A hit by the batter that knocks the ball behind the catcher or off to one side of the field. It counts as a strike against the batter unless he already has two strikes against him.

Fly Ball
A ball hit high into the air. The batter is out if a player on the opposing team catches the fly ball before it hits the ground.

Hit
A batted ball that lets the batter get safely to base.

Home run
A ball hit so far that the batter can run around all three bases and return to home plate.

Pinch hitter
A substitute for a player who was supposed to bat.

Run
Movement around all three bases and to home plate without being put out.

Shutout
A game in which one team does not score.

Stolen base
Movement of a player to the next base as soon as the ball is pitched, without waiting for the batter to make a hit and without being put out by a baseman.

Strike
Failure to hit a good pitch; one that crosses home plate no lower than the batter's knees and no higher than his armpits. This area is called the "strike zone." Also, a foul ball.

Strike-out
Three strikes, which puts the batter out. Also called a "fan" because the batter "fans" the air with his bat.

Switch hitter
A batter who can bat from the left or right side of the plate.

Walk
Movement to first base after the pitcher has thrown four balls. It is also called "a base on balls."

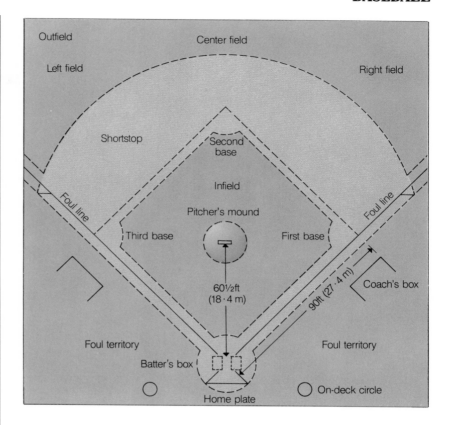

team. The *first baseman*, *second baseman*, and *third baseman* guard the bases. The *catcher* stays behind home plate. He guards the plate and catches the ball when the *pitcher* throws it. The pitcher stands on the pitcher's *mound*, a small hill between home plate and second base. The *shortstop* plays the infield between second and third base. The other three players are the *outfielders*. They are the *right fielder*, the *left fielder*, and the *center fielder*.

Umpires are the officials on the field. They usually wear blue suits and caps. Their job is to decide whether a pitch is a ball or a strike, and whether a player is out or safe. The *manager* of a baseball team is something like a coach. He directs the team and decides which players will be in a game.

When a team is in position on the field, the opposing team is *at bat*. The batter stands in front of the opposing catcher and tries to hit the ball when the pitcher throws it. If he swings his bat at the ball and misses, or if he

Baseball's longest game was between Boston and Brooklyn on May 1, 1920. Darkness ended the game after 26 innings. The score was tied 1-1.

does not swing at a good pitch, he makes a *strike*. But if the pitch is high, low, or off to the side, and the batter does not swing at it, the pitch is then called a *ball*. When a batter makes three strikes, he is *out*. If a pitcher throws four bad pitches, or balls, the batter *walks*, or moves to first base. When the batting team makes three outs, the other team gets its turn at bat.

The batter sometimes knocks the baseball behind the catcher or off to one side of the field. These balls are called *foul balls*. A foul ball counts as a strike, unless the batter already has two strikes. Balls hit *in bounds* are *fair balls*. A *bunt* is a ball hit lightly into the infield. And a ball hit up in the air is a *fly ball*. The batter is out if a member of the other team catches his fly ball before it hits the ground.

Winning a Game A baseball game has nine innings. Both teams have a turn at bat in each inning. A *run* is scored when a player touches all four bases. The team with the most runs at the end of nine innings is the winner. If the score is tied, the teams play extra innings, until one team has a higher score at the end of a full inning.

The object in baseball is for the batter to hit the ball and then reach base. He must reach base before the ball can be picked up, thrown, and caught by the opposing first baseman. A batter may hit the ball so hard that he can run to second or third base before the ball can be thrown to the baseman. He may hit the ball so far that he can run around all the bases and return to home plate. That is a *home run*. When a batter gets to first base, he must move to second, third, and then home. He can do this when

SOME BASEBALL RECORDS

RECORD	PLAYER	TOTAL	DATE
Most home runs in a season	Roger Maris	61	1961
Most home runs in a lifetime	Henry Aaron	755	1954–1976
Highest batting average in a season	Rogers Hornsby	.424	1924
Highest batting average in a lifetime	Ty Cobb	.367	1905–1928
Most strikeouts in a season (pitching)	Nolan Ryan	383	1973
Most strikeouts in a lifetime (pitching)	Nolan Ryan	3,874	1966–
Most stolen bases in a season	Rickey Henderson	130	1982–
Most stolen bases in a lifetime	Lou Brock	938	1961–1979
Most runs in a season	Babe Ruth	177	1921
Most runs in a lifetime	Ty Cobb	2,245	1905–1928
Most games won by a pitcher in a season	Jack Chesbro	41	1904
Most games won by a pitcher in a lifetime	Cy Young	511	1890–1911
Most hits in a season	George Sisler	257	1920
Most hits in a lifetime	Pete Rose	4,204	1962–

the next batter makes a hit. The hit may put the new batter on second. When that happens, the runner (the one that was on first) usually can run around the bases and reach home. That scores a *run* for his team. The other way a runner can move from one base to another is by *stealing* a base. As soon as the ball is pitched, the runner dashes to the next base before a fielder can tag him with the ball to put him out.

A player must do several things well to play good baseball. He must be able to catch the ball when it is thrown or hit to him. He must be able to throw accurately. He must be a good hitter, and he must be a fast runner. The pitcher and catcher work hardest because they are in on every play. The infielders see a lot of action, too. If they are good players, they can make *double plays*. This happens when they throw two opposing players out at the same time. There are also *triple plays*, but they do not happen often. Each person on the team is important to its success, because baseball is a team sport, not an individual sport.

Softball Softball is similar to baseball, but played with a larger ball on a smaller diamond. Despite the name, the ball used is not soft. Softball rules are a little different from those of baseball. For example, the ball must be pitched underhand and there are seven innings in a regular game. The game of softball began as an indoor sport in Chicago in 1888. Today, it is played outdoors as well.

ALSO READ: BALL; GEHRIG, LOU; LITTLE LEAGUE BASEBALL; ROBINSON, JACKIE; RUTH, BABE; SPORTS; SPORTS, PROFESSIONAL.

BASES see ACIDS AND BASES.

BASILICA see CATHEDRAL.

BASKETBALL Basketball is a very popular spectator sport. Dr. James Naismith, a physical education teacher at what is now Springfield College, Massachusetts, invented the game in 1891. It has become one of the most popular sports in the United States and has spread to other countries. The sport is part of the Olympic Games.

Basketball is an important school sport. Both boys and girls play it. Girls' basketball is somewhat different from boys', but it follows the same general rules. Most colleges have basketball teams. Top college players often join professional teams after graduation. Many major American cities have professional basketball teams. Millions of people watch these "pro" teams every year. The Harlem Globetrotters, from New York City, have entertained audiences all over the world with fancy ball-handling and skillful playing.

Playing on the Court Basketball is mainly an indoor activity. The basketball season is during the winter, after football and before baseball. Most high school gyms have at least one basketball *court*. The court is 84 feet (25.6 m) long and 50 feet (15.2 m) wide. The college and professional court is the same width, but it is 94 feet (28.6 m) long. Basketball players under age 15 use another size court— 74 feet (22.5 m) by 42 feet (12.8 m).

At each end of the court is a high, metal hoop with an open-bottomed net hanging from it. This is the *basket* that gives the sport its name. The basket is 18 inches (45.7 cm) wide and 10 feet (3 m) above the floor. Behind the basket is the *backboard*, used to tap a ball into the basket or send it flying wide. The object of the game is to toss, or *shoot*, the ball into the opposing team's basket, or goal. Each team has five players—the *center* (usually the tallest player), two *forwards*, and two *guards*.

▼ *An exciting moment of action in an Olympic basketball game between the United States and the U.S.S.R.*

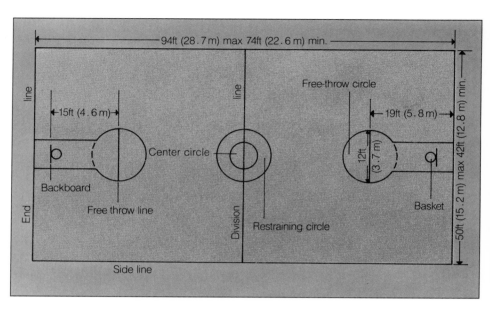

▼ *Basketball players crowd around the basket. This is a sport in which the taller players have some advantages.*

Play starts in the middle of the court, with the two opposing centers facing one another. Each team's forwards guard the other team's guards, and the guards guard the opponent's forwards. An official, called the *referee*, throws the ball up between the two centers. This is called a *jump ball*. Both centers leap up and try to tap the ball to a teammate. When you get the ball, your first object is to move the ball in the direction of the other team's goal. You can do this by *passing*, or throwing, the ball to a teammate. You can also do it by *dribbling*, bouncing the ball while you walk or run down the court. A player cannot hold the ball in the hands while moving down the court. You must pass it to a teammate or shoot at the basket when you stop dribbling.

A basketball player must not commit a *foul* while trying to get the ball from an opposing player. If you do foul, the other team is entitled to a *free throw* at the basket. Holding the ball and pushing another player are fouls. So are body-blocking (stopping another player with your body) and tripping. A player who is fouled may be awarded one or more free throws.

Scoring A basket made during play is called a *field goal*. It adds two points to the team's score. A goal scored by a

free throw counts one point. Free throws are taken from the *free throw line*, 15 feet (4.6 m) from the basket. The winning team is the one with the highest score at the end of the game. The game is a *tie* if both teams finish with the same score. The teams must then play an *overtime* period to break the tie. Overtime periods last for five minutes, except in high school games, when the overtime period lasts for three minutes.

High school basketball games are divided into four *quarters*. Each quarter lasts eight minutes. There is a one-minute break between quarters. The players get a ten-minute rest, called the *half*, after the first two quarters. College games have two 20-minute halves (periods). Professional games are the longest—four 12-minute quarters.

Practice and Fun Height is not too important for young basketball players. But it is a big factor in college and Olympic basketball. And almost all professional basketball players are extremely tall. Kareem Abdul-Jabbar, for instance, stands 7 feet 2 inches (2.19 m) tall.

The tallest player has some advantage. A tall center can easily get the jump ball when the referee starts the game. A tall player does not have to

COMMON TERMS IN BASKETBALL

Field goal
Making a basket during play. It counts two points.

Foul
Breaking the rules of the game. Free throws are given to the opposing team for fouls.

Free throw
Making a throw after a foul by the opposing team. It counts one point.

Jump ball
Throwing the ball up in the air. The referee throws it. Both centers try to tap it to a teammate.

Screening
Blocking an opposing player without touching him.

Dribbling
Bouncing the ball on the floor, using only one hand, in order to take the ball past opposing players and down the court.

Traveling
Holding the ball while moving down the court. A foul.

Rebound
A bounce off the backboard or basket. An unsuccessful shot.

over the ankle and give support.

You do not have to be a member of a high school or college team to play basketball. All you need is a ball and a basket. Many families mount a basket on the side of their house, garage, or barn. Playgrounds often have basketball courts. Any small group of people can play this informal type of basketball.

Basketball is played in more than 1,000 colleges and universities in the United States. There are many intercollegiate basketball conferences, such as the Atlantic Coast Conference, the Big Ten, the Big Eight, the Pacific Eight, and the Ivy League. At the end of the season, many teams participate in holiday tournaments, such as the National Invitational Tournament (NIT) and the National Collegiate Athletic Association (NCAA) championships.

U.S. men professional players compete in the National Basketball Association (NBA), which is divided into Eastern and Western conferences. In professional basketball, a team loses possession of the ball if it fails to shoot within 24 seconds after taking possession. Under NCAA rules, the offensive team must shoot within 45 seconds.

ALSO READ: SPORTS; SPORTS, PROFESSIONAL.

Basketball got its name because James Naismith, in inventing the game, first planned to have square boxes at each end to receive the ball. He couldn't find suitable boxes and made do with two half-bushel peach baskets instead.

reach so high to pop the ball into the basket! If you are tall, you can outreach an opposing player by stretching your arms over your opponent's head. You can catch more high passes. You can also leap up and be the first one to get a *rebound*—when someone shoots, and the ball misses the basket and bounces off the backboard.

Having tall players is not enough to win a basketball game, however. Players must know the rules. They must also know the strategy of the game. This means they must study team plans that often help make baskets. They must move quickly. They must be able to catch the ball well. And they must practice making baskets and passing to teammates.

Body contact—like blocking in football—is not permitted in basketball. Body contact is a foul. So injuries are fairly rare. Basketball players wear rubber-soled shoes that tie up

SOME BASKETBALL RECORDS

Record	Player	Total	Date
Most points scored in one game	Wilt Chamberlain	100	Mar. 2, 1962
Most points scored in one season	Wilt Chamberlain	4,029	1961–62
Most field goals made in one game	Wilt Chamberlain	36	Mar. 2, 1962
Most free throws made in one game	Wilt Chamberlain	28	Mar. 2, 1962
Most rebounds made in one game	Wilt Chamberlain	55	Nov. 24, 1960
Most games won in a season	Boston	82	1985–86
Most NBA championships won	Boston	14	1957–86

From 1959 to 1973, Wilt Chamberlain played in the National Basketball Association (NBA) with the Philadelphia Warriors, Philadelphia 76ers, San Francisco Warriors, and Los Angeles Lakers. He held the record for the most points scored by a player in NBA history (34,419), until it was beaten by Kareem Abdul Jabbar (35,108).

BAT If there were a contest to choose "The Most Remarkable Creature in the World," the bat would have a pretty good chance of winning. Bats look odd, with their mouselike bodies, their big ears, and their strange skin-covered wings. They look even more odd when they sleep, because they hang upside-down, with their wings draped around their bodies. Scientists find them interesting, because in many ways bats are different from all other animals.

For one thing, the bat is the only mammal that flies. Some other mammals, such as the so-called flying squirrel, can glide in the air. But only the bat can fly like a bird. It flies very well, but most bats need a place to take off from. If you put a bat on the ground, it probably would not be able to fly away. It must climb onto something high, like a tree limb or a rock ledge, in order to launch itself into the air. In fact, most bats would be quite helpless on the ground. Their legs are so weak that they can hardly walk.

Unlike the wings of birds and insects, the bat's wings are made of skin. It has short front legs, or arms, and large "hands" with thin bony fingers. The fingers are longer than the bat's whole body. They are covered with a tough *membrane* (a thin sheet of skin) that stretches all the way down to the bat's ankles. There is

▲ *A bat in flight. The wings are membranes of skin stretching from the tips of the bat's fingers down to its feet.*

▲ *The fruit bat or flying fox can be a menace to fruit farmers' crops.*

also a smaller membrane between the bat's feet.

Bats can fly in total darkness and yet never bump into anything! This is because the bat has a built-in "radar system." As it flies, it utters a series of cries that are so high-pitched a person cannot hear them. The sound waves from these cries bounce off objects and echo back to the bat's ears. From these echoes, the bat can tell where the objects are. An old superstition says that bats often try to get caught in the long hair of women. This is untrue. The bat is not at all interested in getting tangled in hair. Its radar system helps it to avoid people's heads as well as other obstacles in its path. It is also not true that bats are blind. They do depend mainly on their ears, but most of them can see in daylight.

Bats All Over the World Scientists have discovered and named over 1,200 different species of bats. They are found all over the world, except in the freezing polar regions. But people hardly ever see them, because they are creatures of the night. During the day they sleep in caves, in trees, or even in houses. Most bats live in hot

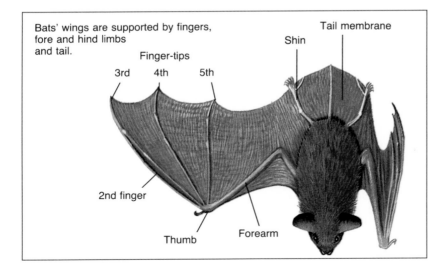

Bats' wings are supported by fingers, fore and hind limbs and tail.

Finger-tips

3rd 4th 5th

Shin

Tail membrane

2nd finger

Thumb

Forearm

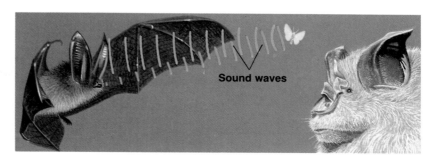

Sound waves

climates. Those that live in cooler lands hibernate during the winter, or migrate to a warmer place.

Most bats are *insect-eaters*. They snatch their meals while flying. Sometimes, instead of using its mouth, a bat will scoop up a flying bug with its wings or with the "basket" formed by the webbing between its feet. Other bats are *fruit-eaters*. But many also eat meat, fish, or nectar from flowers. One kind of bat with unusual eating habits is the sharp-toothed *vampire bat* of Central and South America. It nips the skin of a sleeping animal and then laps up the blood. The victim doesn't even wake up, because the nip doesn't hurt at all. These bats are dangerous to humans only if they carry the disease rabies. Other kinds of bats do not harm people, although fruit-eaters can damage a farmer's orchard. The insect-eaters are helpful, because they feed on harmful insects such as mosquitoes.

The *red bat* of the United States and Mexico gives birth to three or four young at a time. The little fruit-eating *brown bat* is the common cave-dwelling bat of North America. It is only 4 inches (10 cm) long, but its wings spread 10 inches (25 cm). The largest bat is the so-called *flying fox* of Asia and the Pacific Islands. This tree-dwelling bat can have wings as long as 5 feet (152 cm).

ALSO READ: FLYING MAMMAL, MAMMAL, RADAR.

BATTERY A battery is a device that produces electricity. It contains special chemicals that change into other chemicals as it works.

The most common kind of battery is the battery that you put into a machine such as a calculator, digital watch, tape player, or flashlight. It has a steel case with a cap at each end. The two caps are the *terminals* of the battery. One is labeled + (plus, or positive); the other − (minus, or neg-

ative). When properly in place, the terminals press against metal contacts that are connected to a switch in the machine. Pressing the switch completes the electrical circuit and electricity flows from the plus terminal through the machine and back to the minus terminal.

Inside the case of this kind of battery is a mixture of chemicals and a central rod. The chemicals react together. They change into other chemicals, releasing particles of electricity called *electrons* that move to the rod.

When the machine is switched on, the electrons flow from the rod into the machine and back to the case. These moving electrons make up an electric current. The electron flow stops as soon as the machine is switched off or the battery is taken out. But when all the chemicals inside have changed, no more electrons are produced and the battery is dead.

A battery with a single case is called a *cell*. An automobile battery usually contains six 2-volt cells connected together to give 12 volts of electricity. It can be recharged with electricity and used again. Feeding a direct current into the battery changes the chemicals formed back into the original chemicals.

Batteries, even small ones, should be handled with care. Dispose of a battery if there is any leakage of chemicals visible on the case. An automobile battery should be handled only by an adult—*never* touch the chemicals inside it.

ALSO READ: ELECTRICITY.

▲ *How "bat radar" works. The bat squeaks either from its mouth or, like the horseshoe bat (above right), from its nose. Those squeaks are reflected from an insect. Using these echoes as guidance, the bat homes in to catch its prey. Almost all bats have extra-large, sensitive ears.*

▼ *This early battery was invented by the Italian scientist Alessandro Volta in 1800.*

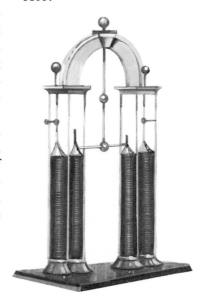

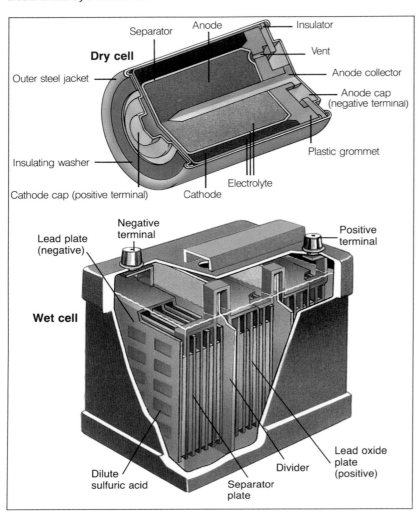

Dry cell

Separator — Anode — Insulator
Outer steel jacket — Vent
Anode collector
Anode cap (negative terminal)
Insulating washer
Plastic grommet
Cathode cap (positive terminal) — Cathode — Electrolyte

Wet cell

Negative terminal — Positive terminal
Lead plate (negative)
Lead oxide plate (positive)
Divider
Dilute sulfuric acid
Separator plate

▲ *A dry cell battery has a chemical mixture surrounding a carbon or copper rod. A wet cell battery has inner cells filled with acid, within a hard protective case. Lead electrodes dip into the acid.*

▲ *L. Frank Baum, American writer of children's stories.*

BATTLES, FAMOUS Wars have played an important part in the history of the world. Certain battles that were not really very important have become important to the countries that fought them. The first battle of the American Revolution, the Battle of Lexington and Concord, is one of these. Nothing was really decided by this battle, but Americans often call it the "shot heard 'round the world." It was not until two years later, when the Americans won the Battle of Saratoga, that the new nation was taken seriously.

Some battles, however, have been "turning points"—they have changed world history. For example, the Persian army of King Darius I tried to conquer Greece in 490 B.C. The Athenian army of 10,000 men, under Gen-

eral Miltiades, met 30,000 Persians at Marathon, a plain about 25 miles (40 km) from Athens. Almost 5,000 Persians were killed in the bloody battle. Fewer than 200 Greeks died, and their grave still stands on the battlefield. The Persians sailed away, and legend says that Miltiades was afraid they would attack Athens before the city learned of his victory. He sent Pheidippides, the army's fastest runner, to carry the news back to the city. The story tells that Pheidippides ran swiftly back to the city, said "Rejoice, we conquer!" and then collapsed and died. The Persians, tired and hurt, did not attack Athens. The Battle of Marathon was one of history's "turning points." By stopping the Persian invasion, it left Greece free to develop into a great civilization. Read more about the other "turning points" shown in the table.

BAUM, L. FRANK (1856–1919) *The Wonderful Wizard of Oz* is a favorite children's book. Its author, Frank Baum, was born in Chittenango, New York. He began writing for a newspaper. His first book was *Mother Goose in Prose*, in 1897. Baum wrote his first Oz book in 1900.

Baum moved to California, where he lived and worked for the rest of his life. He used several *pen names* (names other than his own), and he wrote more than 30 books for boys and girls. But the 14 books about the land of Oz are his most famous.

The Wonderful Wizard of Oz tells the story of Dorothy, a little girl from Kansas. She is blown away by a tornado. Dorothy and her dog, Toto, land in the magical land of Oz. To get home, Dorothy must find the Wizard of Oz, who lives in the Emerald City. The Tin Woodman, the Cowardly Lion, and the Scarecrow join Dorothy in her search.

ALSO READ: CHILDREN'S LITERATURE.

FAMOUS BATTLES

Battle	Date	Who Fought	Why Decisive
Salamis (Aegean Sea)	480 B.C.	Greek and Persian navies	The Persians might have conquered much of Europe if the Greeks had not destroyed half their fleet.
Arbela (modern Iraq)	331 B.C.	Alexander the Great and Darius III	The armies of Alexander the Great defeated the armies of Darius III. Alexander then conquered Persia.
Zama (North Africa)	202 B.C.	Rome and Carthage	The Roman general Scipio defeated Carthage's troops, led by Hannibal. This battle broke Carthage.
Tours (France)	A.D. 732	The Franks and the Moors	Charles Martel, ruler of the Franks, defeated the Moors. This battle stopped the Muslim invasion of Europe.
Hastings (England)	1066	England and France	William the Conqueror, Duke of Normandy, defeated Harold, King of England. Harold was killed and Normans became rulers of England.
Orléans (France)	1429	France and England	Joan of Arc and her French soldiers drove the English out of Orléans. Her victory helped free France of the English invaders.
Lepanto (Mediterranean)	1571	Allied Christians and Turkey	Allied fleet of galleys under Don John of Austria defeated Turkish fleet.
Defeat of the Spanish Armada	1588	England and Spain	Philip II of Spain sent a huge armada of ships to invade England. The English navy and savage storms defeated the armada and Spain lost control of the seas.
Blenheim (Bavaria)	1704	Britain and Austria against France and Bavaria	Allied British and Austrian armies defeated French and Bavarians. Vienna was saved. Territorial expansion of King Louis XIV of France was stopped.
Quebec (Canada)	1759	Britain and France	General James Wolfe defeated French led by the Marquis de Montcalm. Both generals died in this battle of the French and Indian War on the Plains of Abraham outside the city of Quebec.
Saratoga (New York)	1777	America and Britain	British troops under General Burgoyne surrendered to American General Gates. It was the turning point of the Revolutionary War.
Waterloo (Belgium)	1815	Britain, Prussia, Belgium, Netherlands against France.	Soldiers of Britain, Prussia, Belgium, and the Netherlands crushed the army of Napoleon I of France. Napoleon's plan to regain power in Europe was ended.
Gettysburg (Pennsylvania)	1863	Union Army and Confederate Army	Union armies defeated Confederate armies in one of the bloodiest battles of the Civil War. This battle was a "turning point" of the war.
Sedan (France)	1870	Germany and France	The German army invaded France and defeated Emperor Napoleon III. This victory marked the rise of a strong and united Germany.
Marne (France)	1914	France and Germany	The French army stopped a wide German advance at the start of World War I. The Germans lost the chance for a quick victory.
Midway Island (Pacific Ocean)	1942	United States and Japan	This air and naval battle stopped Japan's drive across the Pacific. The United States gained time to build ships and aircraft to defeat Japan in World War II.
Normandy (France)	1944	U.S., France, Britain against Germany	General Dwight D. Eisenhower led an army of three million on "D-Day" to free Europe from German control. This led to Germany's defeat.
Dien Bien Phu (North Vietnam)	1954	France against Viet Minh forces	The French fought a disastrous war and suffered defeat, accepted an armistice, and the Communists controlled North Vietnam under the regime of Ho Chi Minh.

▲ *The Battle of Lepanto, 1571.*

▼ *The sloth bear of India, the Malayan sun bear of east Asia, and the small spectacled bear of South America.*

Sloth bear

Sun bear

Spectacled bear

BAY   see SEACOAST.

BEACH   see SEACOAST.

BEAK   see BIRD.

BEAR   A fat body curled into a ball for a long winter's nap. A pair of playful cubs scrambling up a tree. An angry mother fiercely defending her young. Are these how you think of the large, furry mammals called bears?

Bears look friendly. But they are large, powerful animals. They can be dangerous. You may have heard of hikers in Yellowstone National Park who were horribly injured or even killed by bears. Most bears will attack only if teased or threatened in some way. But all bears, especially the big grizzly, can be dangerous. Never approach a bear and *never* feed or tease one.

The bear is a heavily built animal. Unlike most mammals, it walks with the soles of its feet flat on the ground. This lumbering gait makes bears seem clumsy. But bears can be good runners. Most are also excellent swimmers and climbers. A bear can even take a few steps upright, on its hind legs.

Bears belong to the animal group called *carnivores* (meat-eaters). The larger bears kill and eat animals such as deer or seals. Fish is a favorite food, and bears also eat small creatures such as frogs, mice, and grubs. But they are also very fond of plant roots, berries, and nuts. Honey is a special favorite.

Bears usually live alone. They have poor eyesight, but keen senses of smell and hearing. Those that live in cold northern lands retire to caves during the worst months of the winter. But they do not sleep soundly the whole time, as true hibernating animals do. A loud sound can easily awaken a bear. On warm winter days, a bear may awaken and leave its cave for a short time. Toward the end of the winter, the female bear gives birth to her *cubs* in the cave. Most often, the babies are twins, although sometimes there may be as many as four.

The *brown bears* of North America, Europe, and Asia are among the largest carnivores in the world. They may be up to 9 feet (2.7 m) long and weigh over 1,500 pounds (680 kg). Brown bears include the *Alaskan bear* and the *Kodiak*, which lives on Kodiak Island off Alaska. In spite of their name, brown bears are not always brown. They may be yellowish, black, or tan.

The *grizzly* is one of the best-known brown bears. It may be as much as 8 feet (2.4 m) long and weigh up to 800 pounds (362 kg). Because they are so big and heavy, full-grown grizzlies never climb trees. At one time there were large numbers of these powerful giants in the western United States. But now they are rare, because so many have been shot by hunters. Today, there are only around 1,000 grizzlies, some 200 living in the safety of Yellowstone National Park.

The smaller *black bears* are also found in national parks. They often seem quite tame. A black bear may rush right over to a car stopped on the road and stand with its front paws against the window, waiting to be given a snack. But people should never feed or try to pet these animals. Even a friendly one can suddenly become very dangerous. Other black bears inhabit forests in Asia.

The *polar bear* of the icy North Pole has a heavy white coat that keeps it warm in the freezing cold. Fur on the bottom of its feet keeps it from slipping on the ice. Seals, seabirds, fish, and reindeer are the polar bear's main food. But it also enjoys summer leaves and berries. The polar bear is an excellent swimmer and often travels great distances on floating ice floes.

▲ *Although the brown bear is a carnivore, it also eats berries and other plant food.*

The small *spectacled bear* of South America is only about 2 feet (61 cm) high at the shoulder. It has black and brown hair with lighter circles around the eyes, which make it look as if it were wearing spectacles (glasses). The *Malayan sun bear* of east Asia is a small tree-living bear with orangy-white, ring-shaped marks on the chest. An unusual bear is the *sloth bear* of India. Its snout is long and pointed like an anteater's. Its body is covered with long, shaggy hair, and it has a V-shaped mark on its chest. With its long curved claws, the sloth

bear digs termites from their nests. The claws also help the bear climb trees in search of fruit or honey.

Probably everyone has heard of Smokey the Bear. Most people know him as a cartoon character on posters that teach people how to prevent forest fires. But the cartoon was based on a real black bear that had been rescued from a fire. Smokey lived for many years in the National Zoo in Washington, D.C.

ALSO READ: CARNIVORE, HIBERNATION, MAMMAL, PANDA, POLAR LIFE.

BEARDS AND MUSTACHES
see HAIRSTYLE.

BEAUFORT SCALE   see WIND.

BEAVER
A person who works very hard is often described as an "eager beaver" or a "busy beaver." Indeed, the beaver is a creature of amazing skill and energy. It works constantly at building and repairing its home and getting food.

This large rodent is much more at home in the water than on land. Its plump body, about 2 to 3 feet (60 to 90 cm) long, is covered with coarse brown hair. It has a flat, scaly tail that looks like a paddle. The front feet have sharp claws for digging and carrying, and the hind feet are webbed for swimming. The beaver can hold

▼ *The beaver fells trees by gnawing at the trunk with its large front teeth.*

▲ *A beaver's lodge has underwater entrances. The lodge is built of sticks, grass, and mud.*

its breath under water for as long as 15 minutes. Large, sharp teeth are used to gnaw tender tree bark, the beaver's favorite food. The teeth are also used in felling trees and cutting logs and twigs for use as building materials.

Beavers live and work together in family groups. A pond with a good supply of willow, poplar, and birch trees is the perfect spot for a beaver colony to set up housekeeping. The beavers build their home, called a *lodge*, using sticks and mud. The door to the lodge is under the water, but the living space inside is above water. Beavers often build dams to keep the water of the pond at a constant level. Trees are felled at the water's edge and then gnawed into logs. The beavers carry or drag the logs into the water and float them into place. Then they plaster them together with mud.

There are some beavers in Europe, but most are found in North America. The American beaver has long been hunted for its velvety fur. Early settlers also killed beavers for their meat. Beavers can be a pest, but in many places these busy animals are now protected by law.

The rodent called the *mountain bea-*

ver or *sewellel* of the West is not closely related to the beaver. It is only about 12 inches (30 cm) long, has no tail, and looks more like a muskrat than a beaver.

ALSO READ: FUR, RODENT.

BECKET, THOMAS À. (1118–1170) The churchman Becket played an important part in the conflict between Church and king in England during the 1100's. At first, Becket was a faithful servant of the state. He won the friendship of the young king, Henry II, who made him chancellor (chief justice) of England in 1155. Becket lived a life of wealth and ease at this time. But after becoming Archbishop of Canterbury in 1162, he gave up his luxuries and devoted himself wholeheartedly to the Church. From this time, he and the king began to quarrel bitterly over certain rights of the Church.

▼ *The murder of Thomas à Becket in Canterbury Cathedral, 1170.*

During the Middle Ages, priests who committed crimes were tried by the Church, not by the king's courts. Henry wanted to pass a law to make the clergy subject to royal law. But Becket upheld the rights of the Church. He also resisted Henry's efforts to tax the Church. The quarrel between the two became so serious that Becket had to flee to France for a while. He made the king even more furious after returning to England in 1170. He asked the pope to *excommunicate* (cast out of the Church) the bishops who supported the king's demands. It is said that Henry exclaimed, "Is there no one who will rid me of this turbulent priest?" Four noblemen took him at his word. They went to Canterbury Cathedral on December 29, 1170, and murdered Becket on his way to evening prayers. Pope Alexander III declared Thomas à Becket a saint within three years after his murder.

ALSO READ: ENGLISH HISTORY; HENRY, KINGS OF ENGLAND.

BEDOUIN see NOMAD.

BEE A busy honeybee is one of our best friends. Without it, we would have no honey or beeswax. We could probably not even enjoy such fruits as apples, peaches, and plums. Honeybees carry *pollen* (the yellow powder found in flowers) from one blossom to another. This fertilizes the plants, so they can form seeds for a new generation.

Life in a Honeybee Colony Honeybees are like people; they are *social* animals that live and work together in groups, or *colonies*. Life in a honeybee hive is nearly as complicated as life in a city. In each colony, there are three classes of bees—a *queen*, *workers*, and *drones*. The queen is larger than the other bees. Her job is to lay eggs. The drones are males whose only task is to mate with the queen. Soon after they have done their duty, they die. The busy workers are females, but they cannot make or lay eggs. They are the queen's "ladies-in-waiting." They also build the hive, gather food, make honey, and care for the young.

Inside the hive is a marvelous structure called a *honeycomb*. It is formed from wax, produced by the workers' bodies. The honeycomb is made of many six-sided "cubbyholes" called *cells*. Some cells are used as storage bins for honey and pollen, which the bees eat. The workers collect pollen in little "baskets" formed by the hair on their hind legs. The honey they make comes from *nectar*, a sweet fluid found in flowers. Each worker gathers nectar with her long tongue and stores it in a special part of her body called the *honey stomach*. She puts the nectar into cells. Special chemicals that come from the honey stomach turn the nectar into honey. A worker can "tell" other workers in the hive where a good supply of nectar and pollen can be found. She does this by special kinds of movement called *dances*.

The queen lays her eggs in other cells of the honeycomb. A bee egg is even smaller than the period at the end of this sentence. But each egg hatches into a wormlike *larva*, which grows quickly. At first, the larvae are

Worker

Drone

Queen

▼ *Most bees sting only in defense. The stinger has a barbed tip. After using it, the bee dies. Some bees, such as the African "killer bee," are more aggressive and will sting more readily.*

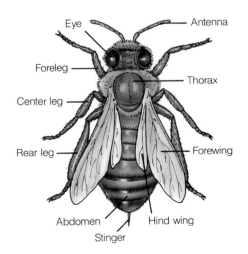
Eye — Antenna — Foreleg — Thorax — Center leg — Rear leg — Forewing — Abdomen — Hind wing — Stinger

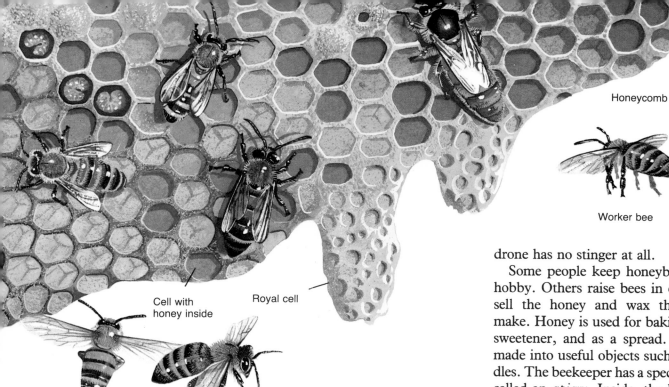

Honeycomb

Worker bee

Cell with honey inside

Royal cell

Honeybee

▲ *A close-up view of a honeybee comb. The comb is made of wax. Each six-sided cell serves either as a nursery or food store. The workers feed pollen or honey to growing larvae while new queens in the "royal cells" are fed special food.*

▼ *Most beekeepers wear netted hats to protect them from stings.*

fed *royal jelly*, a food that comes from the glands in the workers' heads. After a few days, most of the larvae are given *beebread*, a mixture of honey and pollen. But those larvae that are to become new queens are fed only with royal jelly. Each larva becomes a *pupa*. Finally, after 12 days, the pupa becomes an adult.

The body of the adult honeybee has three parts—head, thorax, and abdomen. Two *antennae*, or feelers, are attached to the front of the head. They are used for smelling as well as feeling. The bee's tongue is a long hairy tube used for sucking water, honey, and nectar. The bee's jaws are used for grasping pollen and wax.

The *thorax* supports the bee's six legs and its two pairs of wings. The *abdomen* is the rear part of the body. The worker's abdomen carries a straight *stinger* covered with pointed barbs. Usually the honeybee will only sting in self-defense. When it does, the barbs stick into the flesh of the victim. After loosing its stinger, the bee dies. The queen has a smooth, curved stinger, which she uses only for fighting with rival queens. The

drone has no stinger at all.

Some people keep honeybees as a hobby. Others raise bees in order to sell the honey and wax that they make. Honey is used for baking, as a sweetener, and as a spread. Wax is made into useful objects such as candles. The beekeeper has a special shed called an *apiary*. Inside, the bees are housed in man-made hives.

Other Kinds of Bees Besides honeybees, there are other species of bees. Like the honeybee, the large black-and-yellow *bumblebee* and the *stingless bee* are social insects. Bumblebees are helpful to farmers because they pollinate red clover plants. They also make honey, but it is not used by people. The "stingless" bees actually do have stingers, but they do not use them. Instead, they defend themselves by biting with their jaws. These bees

▼ *A bee gathering pollen from a flower. Many plants are pollinated by these busy insects.*

are found only in tropical parts of the world.

The carpenter, leafcutter, miner, and mason bees are *solitary* insects. They live alone, not in colonies. The *carpenter bee* builds its nest in the twigs or branches of a dead tree. The *leafcutter bee* tunnels in the ground or in soft wood and makes its home with leaves. Eggs are laid in little cups formed by the leaves. *Miner bees* live in underground tunnels. The *mason bee* nests in rotten wood or in an empty snail shell. The *guest* or *cuckoo bee* leaves its eggs in the nest of other bees to be cared for.

ALSO READ: INSECT, METAMORPHOSIS, WASPS AND HORNETS.

BEER see FERMENTATION.

BEETHOVEN, LUDWIG VAN (1770–1827) Beethoven is one of the great composers and also is an important figure in the history of music. He developed new musical forms and he greatly enlarged the repertory for orchestra, piano, voice, and other instruments. He took harmony beyond that of Bach and Mozart. He helped start a whole new kind of music, which is now called "Romantic."

Beethoven was born in Bonn, Germany. His father was a poor court musician. When Ludwig was five he began to study the violin, and he soon took up other instruments. By the time he was ten he was composing his own music. He got his first job, as an organ player, at 12. Four of his compositions were published that same year.

Ludwig grew into a sensitive, moody young music teacher with poor manners and a quick temper. But he was generous and warm-hearted. He made and kept many important friends who forgave his faults. He dedicated many of his compositions to them.

He moved to Vienna, Austria in 1792 and for a time studied with the famous composer Franz Joseph Haydn. Beethoven stayed in Austria for the rest of his life. Unlike other composers who had rich *patrons*, or backers, Beethoven worked alone, a free spirit. He composed symphonies, sonatas, chorales, concertos, quartets, overtures, opera, and much more. Towering over all his compositions are his nine symphonies.

At the age of 27, Beethoven discovered that he was losing his hearing. It was a terrible thing for a musical genius. Beethoven kept his deafness secret for a long time. He became almost totally deaf, and was able to hear his last great works only in his imagination as he put the notes on paper.

ALSO READ: CHORAL MUSIC, MUSIC, ROMANTIC PERIOD.

BEETLE Did you ever see a purple tiger? There is such a creature—but it is not really a tiger. It is a small, fierce beetle. This "tiger" attacks other insects with its jaws.

Perhaps you are more familiar with the ladybug, the firefly, and the weevil. These and thousands of other beetles belong to one of the largest groups of insects. Like the purple tiger, all are good biters, for they have strong jaws, called *mandibles*. Like other insects, they also have three pairs of legs and a pair of feelers. Nearly all beetles have two hard outer front wings, which cover a delicate pair of back wings. Only the back wings are used for flying.

The plump body of a beetle is protected by a brittle, horny shell. The hard front wings form part of this shell. You sometimes find a hard shell of a dead beetle. It breaks with a crunching sound. This shell, like the bones in your body, is the beetle's skeleton. It is an "outside" skeleton, or *exoskeleton*. While many beetles are

▲ *Ludwig van Beethoven, great German composer.*

A bee sting is painful because it contains acid. If you are stung, remove the stinger right away. Wash the spot with soap and water or dilute ammonia, or put baking powder paste on it.

▼ *Most beetles have a similar body shape, and nearly all have their delicate back wings protected by hard outer front wings. Beetles can fly, but many prefer to run about on the ground.*

▲ *A weevil is a kind of beetle with a long snout or beak. For this reason it is called a* snout beetle. *Weevils do great damage to cotton and food plants.*

harmful pests, others are helpful friends because they kill insects that are pests. The polka-dotted ladybug eats aphids and other plant-harming bugs. And some perfectly harmless beetles are colorful creatures that are fun to watch as they crawl or fly around.

Beetle Types   Beetles vary in many other ways besides their importance as friends or foes to people. One of these ways is size. The striped and spotted *Goliath beetle* of Africa is bigger than a mouse, while the lovely ladybug is no bigger than a mouse's eye. Various kinds of beetles make their homes in different kinds of places all over the world. They are found under rocks, behind the bark of trees, in and on all kinds of plants, or even in the underground nests of ants or moles.

The tiny, long-snouted *weevil* lives in farmers' storage bins, where it damages wheat and other grains. A livingroom rug, unfortunately, may be a cozy home and a tasty meal for the young of the *carpet beetle*. These may also be found in closets, happily chewing on woolens or furs. Some beetles live in or on water. The shiny black *whirligig* whirls madly about on the surface of a pond. The *diving beetle* plunges head downward into the water, looking for tadpoles, insects, and little fish to eat.

Many beetles have unusual habits.

▲ *A Colorado beetle and its larvae. These insects can destroy a potato crop.*

The yellow-and-black *burying beetle* buries the dead bodies of small animals. It lays its eggs in the bodies. The *click beetle* is amusing. If you put one on its back, it rights itself with a clicking sound. However, the young of the click beetle are harmful to trees and wooden furniture. The *museum beetle* creeps into the glass cases in museums and munches its way through the bodies of stuffed animals. One of the most fascinating beetles of all is the *firefly*, or *lightning bug*, which is often seen brightening the darkness of a warm summer night. Parts of its body contain chemicals, which produce light that blinks on and off. The beetle uses this light as a signal to attract a mate.

■ **LEARN BY DOING**

You can easily study the life cycle of one kind of beetle, the *mealworm*, and have a constant supply of amphibian or reptilian pet food, too. Buy mealworm larvae at a pet store. Put a few of these wormlike animals in a dry fish tank, along with some dry bran, as food for the young, and some pieces of raw potato, the food for the adults. Sprinkle the bran with water now and then, but don't make it—or the mealworms—soggy.

The larvae will grow about 1¼ inches (3 cm) long. Then they become pupas. The pupas do not eat or

▼ *Not all beetles are pests. In fact, most are useful. The burying beetle is a useful scavenger. It buries the bodies of dead animals as food for its larvae.*

▲ *A scarab beetle, found in dry parts of North America. It has large antennae. If picked up, it squeaks loudly. This beetle is related to the common June bug.*

move about, but their bodies change. Finally, the pupas become adult beetles. The adults lay small oval-shaped eggs from which new larvae hatch. The cycle begins again. How alike, or different, are the larvae, pupas, and adults? How long are newly hatched larvae? Do the larvae or the adults eat more? ■

ALSO READ: INSECT, INSECT PEST, METAMORPHOSIS.

BEHAVIOR see HABIT, INTELLIGENCE, LEARNING.

BEIJING see PEKING.

BELGIUM Belgium is a small country in Europe. It is a bit larger than the state of Maryland. In the north, a plain with 40 miles (64 km) of coast stretches from the Netherlands to France. In the southeast, the Ardennes Forest grows on rocky soil. Belgium is a flat country with numerous cities. (See the map with the article on EUROPE.)

The Belgians are divided into two language groups. The Flemings live in the north and speak a language which is similar to Dutch called *Flemish*. The people in the south are called Walloons and speak a kind of French called *Walloon*.

The Belgians are a hard-working people with a long history of skill in business and manufacturing. The cities bustled with craftsmen and merchants even in the Middle Ages. Belgian goods were sold throughout Europe. In the period from the 1400's to 1600's, Flemish painters perfected the techniques of oil painting.

Because of its location between larger neighbors, Germany and France, Belgium has often been fought over. Julius Caesar conquered the region for Rome about 50 B.C. He defeated the local people, who were called Belgae. It was ruled by Charlemagne in the late 700's, then by the rulers of Burgundy, Spain, Austria, and France. The French emperor Napoleon suffered his final defeat at Waterloo, a few miles from

▲ *The polka-dotted ladybug, or ladybird, beetle has a compact, rounded body. The spots warn birds to keep away, for ladybugs are unpleasant to eat.*

▲ *The click beetle can turn itself over if it lands on its back. It gets its name from the sound it makes when it pops into the air to turn over.*

BELGIUM

Capital City: Brussels (973,000 people).
Area: 11,781 square miles (30,513 sq. km).
Population: 9,900,000.
Government: Constitutional monarchy.
Natural Resources: Coal, farmland, forest.
Export Products: Chemicals, vehicles, machinery, iron and steel, paper, textiles, diamonds.
Unit of Money: Belgian franc.
Official Language: Flemish, French.

▲ *The headquarters of the European Community are in this building in Brussels, Belgium.*

and chocolate. Chief cities are Brussels, Antwerp, Bruges, Ghent, and Liège. The Belgians have learned to be efficient farmers because they have no land to spare. Their main crops are oats, rye, wheat, and potatoes.

ALSO READ: CAESAR, JULIUS; CHARLEMAGNE; EUROPE; EUROPEAN ECONOMIC COMMUNITY; FRENCH HISTORY; NAPOLEON BONAPARTE; NETHERLANDS; ROMANCE LANGUAGES; WATERLOO.

Brussels, the Belgian capital. Belgium became part of the Netherlands in 1815, after the fall of Napoleon. But the Belgians had little in common with the Dutch. They revolted in 1830 and became an independent nation. Belgium was invaded by the Germans and suffered heavy damage in both the world wars of the 20th century, but it is now prosperous again. Belgium is a constitutional monarchy. The monarch is head of state, but laws are made by parliament. Belgium is mainly a manufacturing country and is a member of the European community. It has heavy industry (steel and coal) and also makes textiles, lace, machinery

BELIZE Belize, formerly called British Honduras, is a country on the east coast of Central America. It is only slightly larger than Massachusetts. The land ranges from a flat, marshy coast to heavily forested mountains in the interior. The climate is hot and wet.

Belizeans are descendants of African slaves, Indians, and Europeans. Spanish and English are spoken. Many people cultivate their own small farms and work for lumber companies and plantations.

English buccaneers settled the former capital, Belize City, in the 17th century. Spain later took control and held the territory for 125 years until Britain took it over in 1786. Belize became independent in 1981.

The government consists of a two-house National Assembly and a cabinet headed by a prime minister. Guatemala claims a right to Belize, and following Belize's independence in

BELIZE

Capital City: Belmopan (2,940 people).
Area: 8,867 square miles (22,965 sq. km).
Population: 180,000.
Government: Constitutional monarchy.
Natural Resources: Forest, farmland.
Export Products: Sugar, bananas, citrus, lumber, chicle, fish.
Unit of Money: Dollar.
Official Language: English. (Spanish is also spoken.)

1981, Britain kept a small garrison of troops in the country to help its defense.

ALSO READ: CENTRAL AMERICA.

BELL Bells can be many different sizes and shapes. They are made of metal, glass, wood, and even clay. All are hollow and are struck to make a tone. A bell may be small enough to hold in your hand or large enough for you to stand inside. The Emperor, or Czar Kolokol, Bell in Moscow, Russia, for example, is enormous—it weighs 180 tons (167 metric tons). Whether little or big, most bells are cup-shaped, flaring out at the open end. They may be struck inside by a metal tongue, which is called a *clapper*, or hit on the outside with a hammer.

The earliest bells were wooden. Some were square, instead of round, or beehive-shaped. Ancient peoples made metal bells by pouring hot, melted metal into bell-shaped molds. When the metal cooled, it hardened. Then the mold was removed, and a new bell was finished. This method is still used today.

People began to hang bells in towers long ago and to ring them to tell time, and call others to worship. The bells were rung by hand. Today, most bells are rung mechanically. Modern bells—such as chimes and carillons—do not swing as some church bells do but are "hung dead," meaning fixed in place. *Chimes* are small sets of bells tuned to a scale. *Carillons* are large sets, played from a keyboard by a *carillonneur*. The Netherlands Carillon in Arlington, Virginia, has 49 bells.

Bells are part of the *percussion* (musical instrument that must be struck) section in orchestras and bands. A set of hand-rung tuned bells was too awkward to use, so the *glockenspiel*, a set of metal bars struck with a hammer, was developed to give the same sounds. Small bells on a strap, called *hand bells* or *sleigh bells*, are also used.

■ LEARN BY DOING

You can make instruments similar to bells or chimes. Pour water into wide-mouth jars. Fill each jar to a different level. Tap the jars gently with a spoon to ring the bells. Use several different-size jars. Can you tune them (by adding or pouring out water) to play a musical scale? ■

ALSO READ: BIG BEN, LIBERTY BELL, MUSIC, PERCUSSION INSTRUMENTS.

BELL, ALEXANDER GRAHAM

(1847–1922) On March 10, 1876, Alexander Graham Bell spoke through a strange instrument to his assistant, who was in another room. "Mr. Watson, come here. I want you," Bell said. Thomas Watson heard him and came. The instrument was the first telephone.

Bell was born in Scotland. As he grew up, he learned about voices from his father, who taught the deaf to speak. Bell moved to Canada in 1870 and to Boston in 1871, where he, too, taught the deaf. He later became a United States citizen.

France gave Bell the Volta Prize in 1880 for inventing the telephone. He used the money to set up the Volta Laboratory to do experiments that might help the deaf. He then organized the Volta Bureau, which also helps the deaf. He developed several other devices involving sound and hearing. One was the *audiometer*, which measures a person's ability to hear sounds. Another was a machine to record voices, a phonograph.

Bell was also interested in working with other scientists. He helped spread scientific knowledge by working with the American Association for the Advancement of Science and the National Geographic Society.

ALSO READ: ELECTRICITY, TELEPHONE.

▲ *The giant Emperor Bell in Moscow is the largest in the world. It was cast in 1733 but was cracked by fire in 1737 and since then has never chimed a note.*

▼ *Alexander Graham Bell, inventor of the telephone.*

▲ *Saul Bellow, novelist and Nobel Prizewinner.*

BELLOW, SAUL (born 1915)

One of America's greatest modern writers is Saul Bellow. He was born in Lachine, Quebec, in Canada. His parents had immigrated there from Russia in 1913. When he was nine years old, the family moved to Chicago. After studying at Chicago and Northwestern universities and graduating in 1937, Saul Bellow began a university teaching career, combined with his life as a writer of novels and stories.

The Bellows were a Jewish family, and Saul grew up fluent in Yiddish, a language which had an influence on his English prose style. He won acclaim in 1953 with *The Adventures of Augie March*, which won the National Book Award for 1954. The heroes of Bellow's books are typically bright, intelligent people trying to succeed in a world where their ideals always seem to be thwarted. His books are full of comedy and shrewd observation of people.

Among Saul Bellow's novels are *Henderson the Rain King*, *Hertzog*, and *Humboldt's Gift* (for which he was awarded the Pulitzer Prize in 1976). He won the Nobel Prize for literature in 1976.

▲ *David Ben-Gurion, first prime minister of Israel.*

BEN-GURION, DAVID (1886–1973)

The first prime minister of Israel was David Ben-Gurion. He was born in Plonsk, Russia (now in Poland), the son of Sheindal and Avigdor Green. As a child, he said, "One day I will be the leader of Israel."

He went to Palestine in 1906 to work as a farm laborer. At that time, Palestine was part of the Turkish Ottoman Empire. Young David Green wanted the country to be a Jewish state. He became editor of a weekly Hebrew newspaper, signing his first article Ben-Gurion, which means "young lion."

Ben-Gurion was forced to leave Palestine because he plotted to form a Jewish state. He sailed for the United States. Later, he helped form a Jewish Legion in Canada to fight for the Jews' cause in Palestine. After World War II, Ben-Gurion returned to Palestine to form a secret army. The United Nations in 1947 voted to divide Palestine into Jewish and Arab states. In 1948, at a meeting in a museum in Tel Aviv, Ben-Gurion announced the creation of the new state of Israel.

Ben-Gurion headed the new Israeli government from 1949 to 1953 and again from 1955 until he retired in 1963. He was the minister of defense during the early battles with Arab armies.

ALSO READ: ISRAEL, JEWISH HISTORY, JUDAISM, PALESTINE, UNITED NATIONS.

BENIN

Benin, formerly called Dahomey, is a West African republic somewhat smaller than Pennsylvania. It was made part of French West Africa in the 1890's and was granted its independence in 1960.

Benin is shaped like a long, narrow rectangle, bounded by Nigeria on the east, Burkina Faso and the Republic of the Niger on the north, Togo on the west, and the Gulf of Guinea on the south.

The coast is flat and sandy. A region of lakes and rivers lies inland. Beyond this area is a vast plateau rising to 1,500 feet (457 m). The Atakora mountain range lies in the northwest. The Oueme River, the nation's longest, and the Mono flow southward into the Gulf. The Mekrou and Alibori rivers in the north flow into the Niger River.

Southern Benin is hot and humid, having two rainy seasons a year and two dry ones. The north, however, has two seasons: one wet, one dry.

From about 1500 to 1650, the region was part of the African kingdom

BENIN

Capital City: Porto-Novo (208,000 people).
Area: 43,450 square miles (112,600 sq. km).
Population: 4,550,000.
Government: Socialist republic.
Natural Resources: Oil, forests, hydroelectric power.
Export Products: Cocoa, cotton, palm oil.
Unit of Money: Franc.
Official Language: French.

of Benin, famous for its ivory and bronze sculpture. The kingdom of Abomey (later Dahomey) ruled until the late 1900's. After independence and several revolutions, a one-party socialist government took power in 1972 and held office through the 1980's.

ALSO READ: AFRICA.

BEOWULF Beowulf is the hero of the *epic* (a poem that tells the story of a hero) named after him. The story came from a combination of Scandinavian history, folk tales, and mythology. It took place in Sweden and Denmark. Beowulf was a prince in Sweden who went to Denmark to save the Danes from the monster, Grendel. After a fierce struggle, he killed the monster. But Grendel's mother, another fierce monster, attacked the Danes. Beowulf killed her, too, and later became king.

The poem is the most important writing in *Anglo-Saxon*, also called *Old English*. It was the language spoken in England more than 1,000 years ago. The oldest version of the poem that still exists was probably copied about A.D. 1000 by monks. It is in the British Museum. *Beowulf* may have been first written about A.D. 700.

ALSO READ: ANGLO-SAXONS, FOLK-LORE, LEGEND, LITERATURE, MYTHOLOGY, NORSE MYTH, POETRY.

BERING, VITUS (1680–1741) A sea, an island, and a strait (a water passage), all in the Arctic, are named for Vitus Bering, a Danish explorer. Bering joined the Russian navy when he was a young man. Peter the Great, the Russian czar (king), sent Bering on an expedition to the northern Pacific Ocean.

Bering explored the icy waters east of Siberia, starting in 1727. These waters were later named the *Bering Sea*. This sea is the northernmost part of the Pacific Ocean and the fourth largest open body of water in the world. Bering made an important discovery on his voyage. He sailed through the narrow passage between Siberia and Alaska. He could not see Alaska—less than 40 miles (64 km) away—because of fog. But he did prove that Asia and North America are not connected. The passage is now called the *Bering Strait*. This shallow body of water is frozen much of the year. Scientists think that ancestors of the American Indians crossed from Asia to America—either over the frozen Strait or on a land bridge that later disappeared.

Bering did see the volcano of St. Elias in Alaska on his second expedition, in 1741. But his ship was wrecked on an island. He and many of his crew died there of scurvy. It is now called *Bering Island*.

ALSO READ: ARCTIC, EXPLORATION.

The Bering Strait separating Siberia from Alaska is only 51 miles (82 km) wide. In this channel are two small granite-domed islands, only about a mile (1.6 km) apart. One island belongs to the Soviet Union, the other belongs to the United States. The International Date Line runs between them.

▲ *The Berlin Wall, erected in 1961, divided the city. It was demolished in 1989 as tension between East and West eased.*

▼ *The Brandenburg Gate, one of Berlin's landmarks, now stands in the eastern sector of the city.*

BERLIN The city of Berlin was the capital of Germany until the end of World War II in 1945. Germany lost the war and was divided into two separate countries, the German Democratic Republic (Communist East Germany) and the Federal Republic of Germany (West Germany). Berlin lies within East Germany, about 100 miles (160 km) from the West German border. Berlin was divided, too, into East Berlin and West Berlin. East Berlin, controlled by the Communists, is the capital of East Germany. West Berlin is non-Communist. It has its own government under the supervision of Western nations.

Berlin was badly bombed during World War II. West Berlin was rebuilt, with wide boulevards, tall skyscrapers, and large parks. Elegant stores and theaters now line the *Kurfürstendamm*, West Berlin's most famous boulevard. Visitors come to see the *Tiergarten*, a park with a zoo, a concert hall, and a public meeting hall. Nearby is the *Hansa Quarter*, a modern housing development.

East Berlin looks drab compared to West Berlin. The *Brandenburg Gate* in East Berlin stands near the wall the Communists built in 1961 to separate the two halves of the city. *Unter den Linden*, once the city's grandest boulevard, is in East Berlin. *Marx-Engels Platz* is an immense square.

In 1989, the Berlin wall was torn down amid great rejoicing. Berliners can now pass freely between the two parts of the city.

ALSO READ: GERMANY.

BERLIN, IRVING (born 1888) A boy from Russia grew up and wrote the song, "God Bless America." He was Israel Baline, known to the world as Irving Berlin, composer and writer of many popular songs.

He was born in a small town in Russian Siberia. He came to America with his parents in 1893. They settled in New York City. They were very poor, so Israel and his brothers sold newspapers for pennies.

When he was still just a boy, he became a singing waiter. The first song published with his words (or *lyrics*) earned him 37 cents. He changed his name to Irving Berlin, and began writing tunes as well as words, even though he had never studied music and could barely play the piano. His song "Alexander's

▼ *Irving Berlin, songwriter who made people feel happy. He is seen here in a still from the World War II musical show, This is the Army.*

Ragtime Band," written in 1911, was a hit. Soon he was writing *revues* (shows with skits, songs, and dances), musical comedies, and hit songs that all America sang and danced to. He wrote musical comedies such as *Annie Get Your Gun* and *Call Me Madam*, and nearly a thousand songs. Some of his more famous songs are "God Bless America," "Always," "White Christmas," and "Easter Parade."

ALSO READ: MUSICAL COMEDY, POPULAR MUSIC.

BERMUDA see WEST INDIES.

BERNHARDT, SARAH (1844–1923) Her beautiful voice, the grace of her movements, and her fiery personality made Sarah Bernhardt one of the most famous actresses of her day. She was very thin, with a pale face and frizzy red hair. But she was acclaimed everywhere as "the Divine Sarah."

Her real name was Rosine Bernard. She was born in Paris, France, and was educated in a convent school in nearby Versailles. She later studied acting at the Paris Conservatory. After she became a star in the 1870's, she opened the Sarah Bernhardt Theater in Paris, which she managed until her death. Her best performances were in Racine's classic play *Phèdre*, but they were never so popular as her more sentimental role in *The Lady of the Camellias*, known in America as *Camille*.

In 1914, when Sarah Bernhardt was 70, one of her legs had to be amputated following an accident. After that, she acted from a chair but still performed all over the world. In World War I, she acted for the troops near the front line of battle and was awarded the Legion of Honor.

ALSO READ: ACTORS AND ACTING, THEATER.

BERNSTEIN, LEONARD (born 1918) When Leonard Bernstein was 11, his aunt sent a piano to his house. His family was not musical, but Leonard took piano lessons, and showed such talent that music became his life. He became an internationally known pianist, conductor, and composer.

Bernstein grew up in Boston and studied music at Harvard University. In 1943, the famous conductor Bruno Walter became ill just before a concert of the New York Philharmonic Orchestra. Bernstein stepped in and conducted the orchestra without any practice. He did so well that he became famous overnight. After this, he performed as piano soloist with many orchestras. He also composed music. Some of his most famous works are the *Jeremiah Symphony*, the ballet *Fancy Free*, and the musical *West Side Story*.

Bernstein returned to the New York Philharmonic in 1958 as music director. He was the first American-born, American-trained musician to have this job. He won awards for his television series, *Young People's Concerts*. When he stopped working with the New York orchestra in 1969, he was named the *laureate* (honorary) conductor for life. His *Mass* (1971) was composed in honor of the opening of the John F. Kennedy Center for the Performing Arts in Washington, D.C.

ALSO READ: COMPOSER, MUSIC, MUSICAL COMEDY, ORCHESTRAS AND BANDS.

BETHUNE, MARY McLEOD (1875–1955) Mary Bethune was a leading black educator. As a child, she worked in cotton fields owned by her parents, who had once been slaves. Mary was eager to learn, but for a long time there were no schools for black children in her hometown of Mayesville, South Carolina. Finally, a

▲ *Sarah Bernhardt, French actress.*

▼ *Mary McLeod Bethune, American educator.*

small missionary school was founded, and Mary won a scholarship there. She later won scholarships to a teachers' college in North Carolina and to the Moody Bible Institute. She married a teacher, Albertus Bethune.

Mary Bethune started her own school, in a four-room shack in Daytona Beach, Florida, in 1904. She persuaded leading white townspeople to help support the school. In 1923, Mrs. Bethune's school was joined with a nearby boys' school to form the Bethune-Cookman College.

Mary Bethune was founder and president of the National Council of Negro Women and vice-president of the National Association for the Advancement of Colored People (NAACP). She contributed greatly to the improvement of black education and welfare and to interracial understanding. From 1936 to 1942, she served President Franklin Roosevelt as Director of Negro Affairs.

ALSO READ: NATIONAL ASSOCIATION FOR THE ADVANCEMENT OF COLORED PEOPLE.

BHUTAN Bhutan lies high in the eastern Himalaya Mountains of Asia. This tiny kingdom is about the size of Vermont and New Hampshire together. Tibet lies north of Bhutan, and India is to the south. (See the map with the article on ASIA.) Bhutan is covered by ranges of snowy mountains. Some of the mountains rise more than 20,000 feet (6,000 m). Dense forests of pine and fir cover the slopes. Deer, tigers, and elephants live in the hot, wet jungles of the south.

Most of the Bhutanese people are mountaineers and farmers who live in small tribal villages. They raise cattle, sheep, and yaks in the fertile valleys. The shaggy yak is important for food, clothing, and transportation. Crops must be planted in terraces because the mountainsides are so steep. Bhutan's name means "Land of the Thunder Dragon" because of its mountain storms.

Huge buildings like castles perch on the edges of high cliffs. These are monasteries called *dzongs*, where *lamas* (Buddhist priests) live. Most Bhutanese are Buddhists.

Bhutan is governed by a *maharajah* (ruling prince), who is helped by ministers. Bhutan's large neighbor, India, helps its deal with other countries. Bhutan was shut off from most of the world for many centuries because it had no roads. Today, the country is linked to India by a road network and by airline service.

ALSO READ: ASIA, BUDDHISM, HIMALAYA MOUNTAINS, TIBET.

BIBLE The Bible has been called "the greatest story ever told." It is also known as the *Scriptures*, meaning

BHUTAN

Capital City: Thimphu (20,000 people).
Area: 18,100 square miles (47,000 sq. km).
Population: 1,530,000.
Government: Monarchy.
Natural Resources: Minerals (including limestone, marble, graphite, copper, and coal), forests.
Export Products: Rice, fruit, timber.
Unit of Money: Ngultrum.
Official Language: Dzongkha.

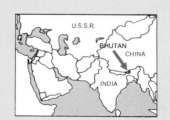

▲ *Part of the Dead Sea Scrolls. These ancient writings, found in a cave beside the Dead Sea, and dating from about 100 B.C., contain the oldest-known versions of the Old Testament.*

"writings." The world "Bible" is the Greek word for "book." The Bible really is made up of many books. These books are sacred, or holy, writings from two religions, Judaism and Christianity. Many people through the years have believed that the Bible is the word of God. There are two main parts, the Old Testament and the New Testament.

Books of the Bible *The Old Testament* tells the story of creation and the history of the ancient Jews, or Hebrews. It was written on *papyrus* (material made from plants) and leather scrolls, between 165 and 122 B.C. Before that, Bible stories had been told aloud for centuries. The 39 books are divided into 3 parts—the *Law*, the *Prophets*, and the *Writings*. The Jews call the five books of the Law the *Torah*. Many people believe that God gave Moses these laws, which include the Ten Commandments. The second part, the Prophets, is about the lives and times of wise men among the Hebrews. The Writings include the Psalms and Proverbs, the Book of Job, and Song of Songs.

The New Testament contains 27 books in three sections, all written between A.D. 50 and 100. They tell about the life of Jesus Christ, his teachings, and his followers. The first section includes the *Gospels*, accounts of the life and teachings of Christ and his followers, and the *Acts of the Apostles*. Events in the time of Christ were passed on mostly by word of mouth. The Apostles were the 12 *disciples*, or followers, of Christ. They wanted to be sure that Christ's teachings would not be lost, so they wrote them down. The *Epistles*, the second part, are letters to Christian communities— encouraging, teaching, and directing them. They were written by the Apostles and other followers of Christ. The third section, the *Book of Revelation*, is a prophecy, or vision of the future.

A third part of the Bible is called the *Apocrypha*. It is the history of the years between the times of the Old and New Testaments. These ten books might be called the fourth part of the Old Testament, but not all religions accept them as holy books. The Roman Catholic, Anglican, and Eastern Orthodox churches accept the Apocrypha. Jews accept only the 39 books of the Old Testament. Most Christians accept both the Old and New Testaments.

The Authorized version of the Bible contains 774,746 words, made up of 3,566,480 letters. The word "and" occurs 46,227 times.

▼ *An illustration of the Genesis story of Noah filling his ark with animals to save them from the Flood.*

መዝጊያ ፨

ኢየሱስም ፡ ይህን ፡ ነገር ፡ በጨ
ረስ ፡ ጊዜ ፡ ሕዝቡ ፡ በትምህርቱ ፡
ተገረሙ ፤

እንደ ፡ ጸሐፎቻቸው ፡ ሳይሆን ፡
እንደ ፡ ባለ ፡ ሥልጣን ፡ ያስተምራ
ቸው ፡ ነበርና ፨

▲ *A page from a Bible written in Amharic, the language of Ethiopia. It is the conclusion of the Sermon on the Mount (Matthew, 7). The Bible has been translated into hundreds of languages.*

History of the Bible The Bible has been published in almost every language. The Old Testament was translated from Hebrew into Greek before the time of Christ. This version is called the *Septuagint*, meaning "70," because 72 scholars were thought to have worked on it. Some of the Bible was written in *Aramaic*, an ancient Near Eastern language. The writers of the books of Daniel and Ezra used Aramaic. The Bible helped keep reading and writing alive even during the years after the collapse of the Western Roman Empire (about A.D. 476 to 1000). Monks living in monasteries during these centuries spent their lives copying the sacred writings. They illuminated (illustrated) their work with gold leaf and brightly colored letters and pictures. They filled sides, or margins, of the pages with delicate designs.

A monk named Jerome translated the Bible from Greek into Latin about A.D. 400. This version was called the *Vulgate*, because Latin was the common (*vulgar*) language of much of the European world. The Vulgate was the Bible of the Catholic Church for many years. John Wycliffe translated the Bible into English for the first time in 1384. Johannes Gutenberg, the German inventor of movable type, printed a famous Bible in 1456. A copy of the *Gutenberg Bible* may be

▲ *The first printed Bibles were produced by Johannes Gutenberg in the 1400's.*

seen today in the Library of Congress.

The Bible was translated into English again in 1582 and 1610. The *Douay Bible* was used by Catholics. The *King James*, or *Authorized Version*, produced by six groups of church people, was published in 1611. It is probably the most famous English Bible and is one of the great works of English literature. The first Bible printed in America, the *Algonkian Bible*, made in 1663, was a translation for Indians. Several new translations of the Bible have been published in this century. Among these are the *Revised Standard Version* in 1952 and 1973, the *New English Bible* in 1961 and 1970, and *The New American Bible* in 1970. These are written in modern-day English. The *Dead Sea Scrolls*, papyrus texts written 200 years before Christ, were discovered in 1947. They have helped scholars make more accurate translations of the Old Testament because

▼ *The Bible story of Jonah and the Whale, in an 18th-century wall painting from a Turkish monastery.*

they are written in the language used by sects of that time.

More copies of the Bible in all its forms have been sold than any other book ever written. The books of the Bible were written by many people, in many different kinds of writing—essays, poetry, history, drama, laws, songs, and prophecies. Daniel in the lion's den, Jonah and the whale, and David and Goliath are inspiring stories of faith. The writers of the Bible meant their work to be used as a guide, as an ideal, for all the peoples of the world who would come after them.

ALSO READ: APOSTLES, CHRISTIANITY, DEAD SEA SCROLLS, JESUS CHRIST, JEWISH HISTORY, JUDAISM.

BIBLIOGRAPHY

BIBLIOGRAPHY There is often a list of other books at the end of a non-fiction book. This list is a bibliography. It tells you that the author of the book studied the books on the list to learn more about the subject. Also, the list will help the reader to find out more about the subject. A bibliography makes it easy to find more information on that subject.

Each book, pamphlet, or magazine article has a separate *entry*, or item, on the bibliography list. Every entry has the same "plan." First, it tells who wrote the book, pamphlet, or article, and what the title is. It then tells the city where the book was published, the name of the publishing company, and the date of publication. Here is a sample entry for a bibliography:

Neal, Harry. *Of Maps and Men.* New York: Funk & Wagnalls, Inc., 1980.

■ LEARN BY DOING

When doing research for an assignment, make your own bibliography. List the books you found useful. And ask your local librarian for help, if you need to. ■

ALSO READ: BOOK, CATALOG, LIBRARY.

BICYCLE People in the United States ride bicycles mostly for fun. But people in many other countries ride bicycles to get where they have to go—to work, to school, or to the market. In some parts of Europe, Asia, and South America more people depend on bicycles than on automobiles. Today's bicycle is a quick, safe way to get from place to place, but this was not always so.

The first bicycle was built in Europe about 1690. The rider sat on a wooden seat and pushed the bicycle along with his feet. This "walking machine" had no brakes, no pedals, and no handlebar. One hundred years later, inventors started working again. An Englishman contributed a gear chain connecting the wheels. A Scotsman attached pedals to the rear wheel of a bicycle, and for the first time a rider did not have to touch the ground. A Frenchman moved the pedals to the front wheels, but the wheels were made of iron and people called his bicycle the "boneshaker" because it was so uncomfortable to ride.

Bicycles were becoming popular. They still, however, did not look like bicycles of today. The front wheel was as tall as a man, and the rear wheel was quite small. Then, in 1885,

When pedals were first fitted to bicycles, cycling became an instant success. But there were not enough bicycles to go around, so special rinks were built where people could hire a "boneshaker" for one cent a minute.

▲ The dandyhorse or draisine of 1817 looked like a bicycle but had no pedals.

▼ The "ordinary" or highwheeler bicycle of 1883 had a huge front wheel. The rider needed a special mounting step to get on it.

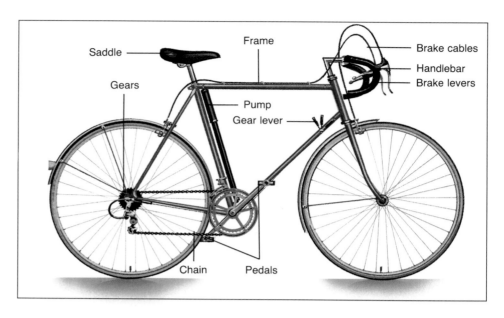

J. K. Starley of Great Britain made a bicycle with both wheels about the same size. With the addition of air-filled rubber tires and a chain-driven gear, bicycles became comfortable, safe vehicles, which were soon being ridden by many people.

Bicycle racing became a recognized sport in the 1890's. Today races are held on indoor and outdoor tracks, with steeply banked curves and short straightaways. Even more exciting are the major road races, held mainly in Europe. The best racers compete in the *Tour de France* each year, traveling more than 3,000 miles (4,800 km) in about three weeks. In 1986 an American rider, Greg Lemond, won the Tour de France—the first win by a U.S. competitor.

The sport of racing has produced bicycles that have made riding easier today. Very light, aluminum, 10- or 12-speed bicycles are common. They originally were used only by serious racers.

For most people, bicycling is just fun in the open air, whether exploring the byways or rambling through the countryside. Bicycling is a good way to tour the U.S. and other countries. Bicycle tourists either camp out overnight or stay at inexpensive lodgings called *youth hostels*. Today, people are aware that bicycles are a good means of transportation. Bicycling keeps you fit and does not add to air pollution or noise problems.

▼ *Cyclists from all over the world take part in the Tour de France, a test of endurance for both rider and machine.*

BIG BEN   One of the most famous sights in London, England, is a clock tower attached to the Houses of Parliament. In it is a huge bell called Big Ben. It weighs 13½ tons (12.2 metric tons). Members of Parliament named it after Sir Benjamin Hall, a large man who was Commissioner of Public Works when the bell was installed in 1859.

The name "Big Ben" is now used also for the giant clock on the Parliament tower. The hour hands are 9 feet (2.7 m) long, and the minute hands are 14 feet (4.3 m) long. Lord Grimthorpe, a lawyer, designed it. The Big Ben clock is usually very accurate. But once it did lose five minutes—when a flock of starlings settled on one of its hands.

BILLIARD GAMES Billiards is a game for two or four players. It requires good coordination and many hours of patient practice. Some historians believe billiards was developed in England more than 600 years ago, in an attempt to make lawn bowling an indoor game. Early colonists from England, France, and Spain brought the game with them to America. Gradually the equipment and rules became established.

The game is played on a special table made of slate and covered with green felt. A standard table is 5 feet (152 cm) wide and 10 feet (305 cm) long. The sides of the table above the flat surface are padded with rubber and are called *rails* or *cushions*.

There are three billiard balls. One is red. The other two are white. One of the white ones has two red dots on it. A player uses a *cue* (a long wooden stick) to hit the cue ball, one of the white ones. He makes a point if his cue ball touches the other two balls before it stops rolling. A game is usually 50 or 100 points.

A popular variation of billiards is *pocket billiards*, or *pool*. The players use the same kind of cue sticks. The table is similar, but it is smaller and has six pockets, one in each corner and one halfway down each long side.

Pool players use 15 numbered balls and one cue ball. The cue ball is white, and the numbered balls are different colors. Balls 1 through 8 are solid colors, each with its number showing. Balls 9 through 15 are white with colored stripes, and the numbers are on the stripes. The object in most pool games is to hit the cue ball into the other balls and knock them into the pockets, without the cue ball's falling in.

The game known as *snooker* is popular in Britain, Canada, and Australia. Snooker is played with 22 balls: one white (which is the cue ball), 15 red, and six colors. The colors are valued by the points they score when knocked into a pocket. A red ball scores 1, yellow 2, green 3, brown 4, blue 5, pink 6, and black 7. Each player tries first to knock a red ball into a pocket, followed by one of the colors, followed by another red, and so on. Each red pocketed stays off the table, but colors are put back until all reds have been removed.

ALSO READ: GAMES.

▲ *Chimes ring out from Big Ben, one of the world's most famous clocks. Its bell is heard hourly around the British Houses of Parliament in London and is carried around the world on BBC overseas radio broadcasts.*

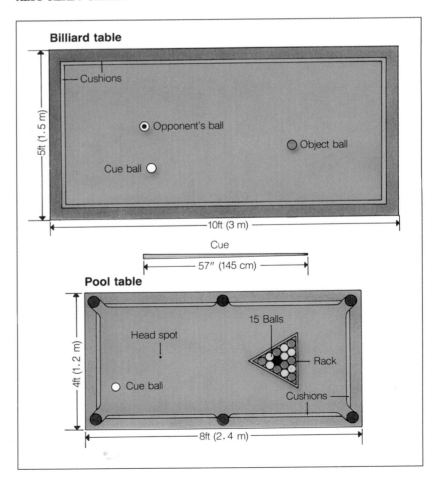

Billiard table

Cushions

5ft (1.5 m)

⊙ Opponent's ball

○ Object ball

Cue ball ○

10ft (3 m)

Cue

57" (145 cm)

Pool table

Head spot

15 Balls

4ft (1.2 m)

○ Cue ball

Rack

Cushions

8ft (2.4 m)

Decimal	Binary
1	0001
2	0010
3	0011
4	0100
5	0101
6	0110
7	0111
8	1000

▲ *The binary system uses only two numerals, 0 and 1. The table above shows some decimal numbers and their binary equivalents. The decimal number 7, for example, is written 0111—1 one, 1 two, 1 four, no eights. All computers work in this way, by simply counting 0s and 1s.*

▼ *This diagram shows the proportion of the chemical elements that make up the human body.*

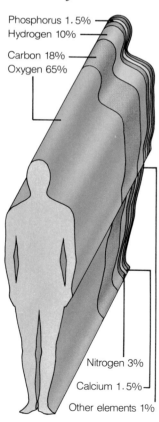

Phosphorus 1.5%
Hydrogen 10%
Carbon 18%
Oxygen 65%
Nitrogen 3%
Calcium 1.5%
Other elements 1%

BILL OF RIGHTS The first ten Amendments to the Constitution of the United States are also called the Bill of Rights. Most of these rights protect the individual citizen against the government. Laws passed by Congress in conflict with the Bill of Rights may be overruled (declared unconstitutional) by the United States Supreme Court.

The rights guaranteed in the first ten Amendments are rights that the English had earned over many centuries, beginning with the Magna Carta in 1215. Some of the rights had been written into the charters of the various colonies. When the U.S. Constitution was completed in 1789, many people wanted the rights included so that the Federal Government would not become too powerful. The Constitution was accepted by the states with the understanding that Amendments, stating the rights of the people, would be made promptly. The ten Amendments making up the Bill of Rights were added in 1791.

The first Amendment forbids the government to interfere with freedom of speech, freedom of the press, and freedom of religion. The Amendment also guarantees the right to ask the government for justice and to demonstrate peaceably. The second Amendment says that citizens have a right to possess arms (weapons). The third Amendment says that citizens cannot be forced to provide room and board for soldiers in their homes. The fourth guarantees that people or their property cannot be searched or taken away without a warrant (permission) that has been issued by a law officer.

The fifth, sixth, seventh, and eighth Amendments have to do with fair and just treatment in the courts of law. A person cannot be tried twice for the same crime and cannot be forced to testify (speak out) against himself. He or she must be tried by a jury if desired, and the trial must be held in the area where the crime was committed. He or she must not be given cruel and unusual punishment.

The ninth Amendment says that other rights not specifically mentioned in the Bill of Rights or the Constitution belong to the people. The tenth Amendment provides that powers not given specifically to the Federal Government shall belong to the States and the people.

ALSO READ: CIVIL RIGHTS; CONSTITUTION, UNITED STATES; COURT SYSTEM; FOUR FREEDOMS; STATES' RIGHTS.

BINARY SYSTEM Because we have ten fingers our number system grew up on a *base* of ten—the *decimal system*.

In our decimal system the value of each number changes according to its position in the figure as a whole. For example, the numerals 2 and 6 can give the figure 26. If we turn them around we get 62. The numerals are the same but their position makes all the difference. You multiply a number by 10 by moving it one place to the left. The numeral 1 by itself is just 1. Move it one place to the left and it becomes 1 times 10, or 10. Move it another place to the left and it becomes 100, and so on.

In the binary system, when you move a numeral one place to the left you multiply its value by two. A 1 by itself is 1. Move it one place to the left and it becomes 1 times 2, or 2. It is written 10. Move it another place to the left and it becomes 1 times 2 times 2, or 4. This is written 100. Any number can be written in binary. The number 18 is 10010.

ALSO READ: ARITHMETIC, COMPUTER, DECIMAL NUMBER.

BIOCHEMISTRY All living things are made of tiny blocks of matter called *cells*. The activities that mean "this object is alive" take place in the cells. The activities are mainly chemical changes, and they occur in different ways in different living things. Biochemistry is the study of the chemical reactions that occur in the cells of all living things.

Biochemists seek to know how living things grow. They have traced the way we digest food and how the food is chemically burned to release energy. They have followed oxygen from the air to the cell, where it is used to burn food. They have discovered substances called *enzymes* and *hormones*, which direct how the cell will use the energy. From this work, scientists have been able to learn what kinds of food make people healthy. They have learned the value of calories, vitamins, and minerals. They have developed medicines that help cells do their work properly.

In recent years, biochemists have been studying special molecules in the cell, called *nucleic acids*. The nucleic acids are very complex, and scientists have found that they control all growth and reproduction. One form of nucleic acid—RNA (ribonucleic acid)—is found throughout the cell, where it controls protein-making. DNA (deoxyribonucleic acid), another form of nucleic acid, is found only in the nucleus. It carries and passes a kind of "blueprint" of the plan of a living thing from one generation to the next in the form of *genes*. It is the substance that makes you a human being but different from any other one.

Biochemistry is one of the most exciting sciences today. New questions are popping up in biochemists' laboratories everywhere. What causes some mental illness? What can prevent birth defects? How does the diet of a poorly fed child affect intelligence? Answers to these and a thousand other questions are being pieced together one step at a time by biochemists.

ALSO READ: CELL, DIGESTION, ENZYME, GENETICS, HORMONE, GROWTH, LIFE, RESPIRATION.

BIOGRAPHY   The written story of a real person's life is a biography. *What* happened, and *where* and *when* events took place are important parts of any biography. But facts alone can be dull. A biography can, and should, read like an adventure story.

In times past, biographies were often written to teach a lesson. These were called *didactic* biographies. Sometimes, the facts in these books were exaggerated. For example, the famous biography of George Washington, written about 1800 by Parson Weems, told the story about George chopping down his father's cherry tree. This old tale was not true. Another fault of some older biographies was their "perfect" image. Authors left out important facts about a person if they were not flattering.

A good biography of today tells as many facts, good and bad, as possible.

■ **LEARN BY DOING**

Interview a parent or friend, and then try to write a short biography of him or her. Remember, you, as author, have two jobs—to give the facts and to make them interesting. Can you avoid putting your own opinions into the story? ■

ALSO READ: AUTOBIOGRAPHY, DIARY, LEGEND, LITERATURE.

BIOLOGY   More than a million different kinds of animals and over 330,000 different kinds of plants live on Earth. The science that studies all these living organisms and their relationship to each other is biology. It is the science of life.

Biologists place every known organism into one of three large groups, called *kingdoms*. The two largest of these kingdoms are the *Plant Kingdom*, containing all plants, and the *Animal Kingdom*, containing all ani-

▼ *Four stages in the evolution of the horse, from about 55 million years ago to some 5 million years ago.*

Eohippus (dawn horse)
55-40 million years ago

Mesohippus
40-25 million years ago

Merychippus
25-10 million years ago

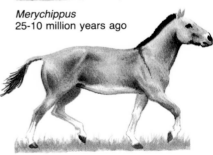

Pliohippus, the ancestor of modern horses, asses, and zebras

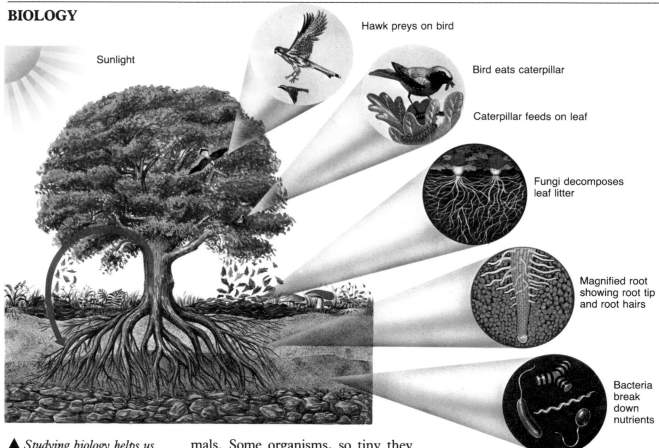

Sunlight

Hawk preys on bird

Bird eats caterpillar

Caterpillar feeds on leaf

Fungi decomposes leaf litter

Magnified root showing root tip and root hairs

Bacteria break down nutrients

▲ *Studying biology helps us understand how living things relate to one another and to their environment. Plants turn sunlight into energy, and this energy is passed on to plant-eating animals. In turn, plant-eating animals (such as caterpillars) are eaten by other animals (songbirds), which may in turn be eaten by higher predators (hawks). In this way, the energy is passed along a food chain. When animals die, their bodies decompose (break down) into particles that mix with the soil, so the energy is reused by plants. In this picture, the oak tree's roots absorb nutrients from the soil. The blue arrow shows how dead leaves from the tree are broken down by fungi and bacteria. The tree's root hairs help the tree to absorb nutrients, giving it energy to grow new leaves. And so the cycle goes on.*

mals. Some organisms, so tiny they can only be seen with a microscope, do not act exactly like plants or animals. Biologists group these particular living things into the *Protist Kingdom*. *Zoology* is the study of only the members of the Animal Kingdom. *Botany* is the study of the Plant Kingdom. *Taxonomists* are biologists whose special work is to group living things into their proper kingdoms and subgroups.

Some biologists are not zoologists or botanists—they study both plants and animals. Every living thing is made up of cells. *Cytology* is the study of cells, what they look like and how they function (work). Cells fit together in structures that give daisies, pigeons, people, and all other living things their special shapes. The study of the structure of living things is *anatomy*. All living things have functions such as digestion, growth, respiration, and reproduction. *Biochemistry* and *physiology* are studies of these functions. Diseases can cause living things to stop functioning or to function inefficiently. *Pathology* is the

study of how diseases affect living things and what can be done to prevent and cure disease.

Why do some people have blue eyes and others brown ones? Why is every person, cow, and oak tree different from every other person, cow, and oak tree? *Genetics* is the study of these differences. How can so many different kinds of living things exist in the world at once? In how many different ways do all these organisms depend upon one another for survival? These questions and many others are answered by *ecology*.

Still other biologists study theories of *evolution*, the idea that change affects living things over millions of years. About 60 million years ago the ancestors of horses were only as big as dogs. For what reason have these animals grown larger? This is a question that the study of *evolution* tries to answer.

■ LEARN BY DOING

Biologists have many other special studies, such as *paleontology* (the study of fossils) and *space biology* (what happens to living things in space). You can get an idea of how many different kinds of subjects biologists are studying from the table. And you can find out about many of the problems biologists want to solve in the articles listed below. ∎

ALSO READ: BACTERIA, BIOCHEMISTRY, BOTANY, CELL, ECOLOGY, EVOLUTION, FOSSIL, GENETICS, LIFE, PARASITE, PHYSIOLOGY, PROTIST, ZOOLOGY.

BIOLUMINESCENCE Many types of living organisms have the ability to glow in the dark, or *luminesce*. The process producing this light is called bioluminescence. It produces cold light of various colors, by means of chemical reactions inside the organism. Light is produced when *enzymes* break down a substance called *luciferin*. Bioluminescence is responsible for the flashing tail lights of the firefly, used to attract a mate, and for the brilliant lights of many deep-sea fishes. These lights help the fish to find other fish in total darkness and to find food. Light is produced in special organs, arranged so that the pattern of light is easily recognized by other creatures.

Some types of marine *plankton*, tiny floating animals and plants, luminesce brightly when the water is disturbed by a swimmer or a boat. Many *bacteria* and *fungi* also produce light by bioluminescence. The same chemical process has been copied by chemists to produce cold lights that are used for emergency lighting. These lights glow brightly until the light-producing chemicals are used up.

ALSO READ: DEEP-SEA LIFE.

BIRD The world has about 9,000 kinds of the feathered creatures called birds. About 800 species (kinds) live in North America alone. One of these is the tiny hummingbird, which weighs not much more than three sheets of typewriter paper. North America's tallest bird is the whooping crane. It stands about 5 feet (1.5 m), and has a wingspread of 90 inches (2.3 m). It is one of the rarest birds in the world.

The many different kinds of birds in the world all belong to a class in the animal kingdom known as *Aves* (Latin for birds). This class is then divided into smaller groups, known as *orders*. Most *ornithologists* (scientists who study birds) recognize about 28 orders of living birds.

Many ornithologists start the grouping of birds with the orders that are extinct and are found only as fossils. The next orders of birds are those that do not fly but can walk, run, or swim. (Some, like penguins, can walk and swim.) The flying bird orders complete the classification. Of the flightless birds, the best known examples include the ostrich, emu, kiwi, and rhea The moa of New Zealand belonged to this group but is now extinct. A penguin does not fly but instead uses its wings to help it swim underwater.

Most birds can fly. It is the marvel of flight that makes them unusual among the warm-blooded animals. Have you wondered why birds (almost alone among the warm-blooded

SOME BIOLOGICAL SCIENCES
Evolution Study of the process of change in living creatures
Biosociology Study of the environments of groups of living things
Paleontology Study of fossils
Parasitology Study of parasites
Anatomy Study of the structures of plants and animals
Bacteriology Study of bacteria
Embryology Study of the formation and development of living things before birth
Genetics Study of heredity
Ecology Study of the relationships between living things and their environments
Cytology Study of cells

▼ *A female firefly glows to attract a mate —an example of bioluminescence.*

▼ *A baby harrier or marsh hawk waits for food. Most young birds are fed by their parents while in the nest.*

A peacock's call is so loud that it can be heard very far away. It sounds like a woman screaming. This call is so frightening that many peoples have believed that peacocks are unlucky.

Birds have to learn to sing. Young birds that are reared away from the company of their own kind never produce the true song of their species. Even in their natural surroundings it takes some time before birds learn all the correct notes.

▼ *The kind of bill, or beak, a bird has is a clue to the kind of food it eats.*

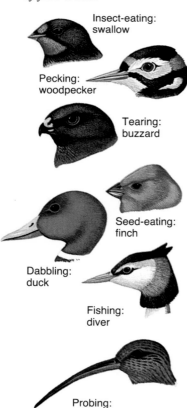

Insect-eating: swallow

Pecking: woodpecker

Tearing: buzzard

Seed-eating: finch

Dabbling: duck

Fishing: diver

Probing: curlew

animals) can fly? It is because birds have feathers; wings; a breastbone with a special ridge of bone called the *keel*; strong muscles; hollow, but strong, bones; a brain largely used for seeing, hearing, and motion control; and even specialized breathing organs. The bird's whole body is designed for flight. All these special body organs must be present and work together for a bird to fly. The birds we know today probably developed (evolved) from ancient reptiles many millions of years ago. The oldest known birdlike creature, called *Archaeopteryx*, had a skeleton like a reptile, with a vertebral column that extended into a tail. Notice that birds still have scaly feet like reptiles.

Flight is thought to have developed in this way: First, birds ran swiftly. Next, they were able to make long, wing-flapping leaps. Perhaps some leaps were "glides" from a high tree to one not so high. Finally, birds were able to fly. True flight took a long, long time to develop.

Where Birds Are Found Birds are able to live in most parts of the world. Penguins live in Antarctica, the icy region around the South Pole. The equator is home to many species of brilliantly colored tropical birds. A species of quail is found in the desert. The albatross, a true sea bird, stays on or above its watery habitat for months at a time, without ever coming to land. The water ouzel, or dipper, of the American West is a stream resident. It actually runs along a streambed at times, looking for food.

Some birds are found in different places at different times of the year. Both the tiny hummingbird and the huge whooping crane make long flights (*migrations*) twice a year. They fly north each spring to mate and raise their young. In the fall, they fly south to pass the winter. Some birds fly thousands of miles between their winter and summer homes. The golden plover nests far north in Arctic tun-

dra. It winters in southern South America, more than 7,000 miles (11,000 km) away. At the same time, its *plumage* (feathers) changes from dark colors to lighter colors. Most birds migrate to find the same kind of environment for winter and summer.

Ways of Life Every bird has its place in nature. It has its very own *ecological niche* (place in the plant and animal community). Some birds are *predatory*, meaning they kill other animals for food. The golden eagle is a predator; it kills rabbits and rodents. Hawks and owls prey on rats, mice, and some insects. Predators help to reduce the number of rodents and control the damage done by rodents to crops and stored foods. Diving ducks plunge to depths of 30 feet (9 m) for the plants they eat. Thrushes are the greatest eaters of insects. Bluejays and cardinals are seed-eaters. Geese eat grass and seeds. And hummingbirds drain nectar from flowers. The feet and beaks of birds vary with the way the animals live.

■ LEARN BY DOING
You can attract hummingbirds to your garden. Make, or ask an adult to make, a sugar and water syrup. Find a test tube from a chemical set or a plastic medicine bottle. Make sure it is absolutely clean. Get some fine wire and a long, slender stick (bamboo, if you can find it). Wire the test tube to the top of the stick, slantwise. Tie a bit of red cloth around the opening of the test tube. Stick the pole with its test-tube feeders into the ground. Fill the test tube with sugar water.

If you live in the East, you will probably attract the ruby-throated hummingbird. This species is the only hummingbird found in eastern North America. In the West, and elsewhere in the Americas, you will attract a great variety of hummers. ■

Many birds receive their common names because of their habits. The

▶ *Birds fly either by flapping or gliding. A bird's wings produce "lift" because of their shape. As it comes in to land, a bird uses its tail as a brake, spreading its feathers for greater control during the landing. Flying birds have lightweight bodies but amazingly strong muscles.*

▶ *The flamingo's long legs are fine for wading in lagoons. It sticks its long neck under water and uses its specially curved bill to sift out water creatures from the mud.*

turnstone, for example, is a shorebird with orange-colored legs that turns over pebbles as it walks along the beach. The bobwhite (common quail) gets its name from its call. The honeyguide of Africa leads both people and badgers to trees in which there is wild honey. The burrowing owl often makes use of the burrows made by prairie dogs.

Nests and Eggs Some birds have little or no need for nests. Others build elaborate ones. The "nest" of some penguins is nothing more than a bare rock. A depression in the ground, lined with wild grasses, seems to satisfy the wild turkey. The mound-building birds of Australia scrape together piles of leaves and twigs. The small bushtit hangs grass pockets on branches. And the cowbird does not bother with any form of nest. The female lays her eggs in the nest of another species when the rightful owner is away. Some orioles build large community "apartment house" nests.

The number of eggs a female bird lays depends upon the species. Petrels

◀ Cranes are the largest of all wading birds, with long necks and long heads. Many cranes are migrants, traveling long distances. The North American whooping crane is one of the continent's rarest birds.

▼ A mute swan. Swans are large, handsome birds related to ducks and geese. They have webbed feet and swim around, feeding on water plants.

▲ Hummingbirds are the only birds that can fly backwards! Their wings beat so fast you can only see a blur of movement.

Great gray shrike

▼ Owls are night hunters and have excellent eyesight and hearing. They fly almost silently, pouncing on their prey, which includes mice, voles, and other small animals.

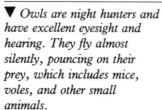

Lesser gray shrike

▲ Crowned pigeons belong to the group of land birds that hunt for food on the ground. They bob their heads while walking. The city pigeon is another member of this group.

▲ Shrikes are named after their piercing calls. They have the habit of sticking their food on thorns and are also known as butcherbirds.

◀ The great spotted cuckoo belongs to a family of birds that lay their eggs in the nests of other birds. When the young cuckoo hatches, it is fed and cared for by its foster-parents.

◀ The booby or gannet is a diving bird of the seacoast. These birds dive headlong into the water to catch fish.

▶ The ostrich is the largest of all living birds, at 8 feet (2.5 m) high. Shown here are a male (right) and female.

lay only a single egg. It is usually white and is deposited in a nest of grass and twigs. Sometimes the egg of the storm petrel is lightly marked with purple. European widgeons lay seven or eight buff-colored eggs. American widgeons, or baldpates, may lay as many as 18 eggs, though the average is 10. Many birds lay three, four, or five eggs.

Hazards of Bird Life Young birds face dangers. They may be prey for snakes, mammals, or even other birds. The nest of a perching bird may be a long way from the ground, and it is easy to fall out of. One of the great dangers to waterfowl is a long, dry, hot spell. The drainage of marshes ruins the habitat of marsh-dwellers such as bitterns, marsh wrens, and red-winged blackbirds.

Adult birds, too, face dangers. Strong light confuses night-flying birds, causing them to crash against obstacles. Birds that migrate at night, including many favorite songbirds, are sometimes killed flying into television towers and other tall structures, or even airplanes. Heavy storms, diseases, and predatory animals are also bird killers. And today, pollution, such as oil spills at sea, is responsible for many bird deaths.

Many birds in North America are protected because lands have been set aside for them. These lands, called National Wildlife Refuges, provide life's essentials for many birds. Some states have laws protecting songbirds. All states regulate the hunting seasons on non-migratory birds. The Federal Government administers the laws protecting migratory birds. And treaties with Canada and Mexico protect more than 50 different species. Even so, there are many birds that are in danger of becoming extinct. The huge California condor has become so rare that efforts are being made to rear chicks in captivity to save the species from dying out. The Everglades kite, rare already, came even closer to

extinction in 1971 when its Florida home went through a long, dry period. Even the national bird of the United States, the bald eagle, is becoming scarcer and scarcer. The bald eagles, with white feather caps on their heads, have been shot illegally and poisoned by harmful chemicals used by farmers. So now people are doing their best to protect the eagles.

For further information on:
Ecology, *see* ANIMAL HOMES, CITY WILDLIFE, ECOLOGY, MIGRATION, WILDERNESS AREA.
Land Birds, *see* BIRDS OF PREY, FLIGHTLESS BIRDS, GAME BIRDS, GARDEN BIRDS, HUMMINGBIRD, OWL, PARROTS AND PARAKEETS, PIGEON, POULTRY, STORK.
Water Birds *see* CRANE, DUCKS AND GEESE, GULLS AND TERNS, PELICAN, PENGUIN, SEABIRDS, WATER BIRDS.
Zoology, *see* ANIMAL DEFENSES, ANIMAL KINGDOM, ANIMAL VOICES, EGG, EVOLUTION, FEATHER, HANDS AND FEET, SKELETON.

▲ *The bald eagle is America's national bird. It actually has a well-feathered head, the white feathers giving the "bald" look.*

BIRD WATCHING see NATURE STUDY.

BIRDS OF PREY Some birds feed on small animals and other birds. They are called birds of prey. They help to control the number of small birds and animals. These birds form

▶ *Birds of prey, such as this goshawk, have the keenest eyes of any bird. These birds strike their prey with their powerful feet, or talons. The hooked bill is used for tearing flesh when feeding.*

Golden eagle

Sparrowhawk

Tawny owl

▲ *Three representative birds of prey. The golden eagle is a bird of the mountains. The sparrowhawk hunts around farmland and woodland. The tawny owl, like most owls, is a nocturnal (night) hunter.*

one large *order* (group) of birds. Several kinds of birds are included. All of them are flesh-eaters with sharply hooked, curved bills, and strong, sharp, curved claws. Most of them eat only meat, but some eat vegetables, too. Owls are not included in the same order, but they are also flesh-eating hunters.

Wing shapes tell how birds of prey hunt. Birds with long, narrow wings fly fast. They capture their prey in the air. Those with short, rounded wings can turn sharply. They attack close to the ground where they can corner their prey. Birds with broad wings soar high above the ground. They usually feed on *carrion* (dead animals).

Eagles and Falcons   *Bald eagles* and *golden eagles* are the only eagles found in North America. They are America's largest birds, except for the California condor. The bald eagle is not really bald—its head and neck are covered with pure white feathers. Bald eagles live in the mild-climate areas of North America. Males weigh up to 8 pounds (3.6 kg) and have a wingspread of 7 feet (2.1 m). Females are larger, up to 12 pounds (5.4 kg). The bald eagle is the national bird of the United States, but it is very rare because many of these birds have been shot by hunters. Also, a high concentration of DDT (a chemical used to kill insect pests) in eagles has made them lay thin-shelled eggs that do not hatch. The golden eagle lives in the mountains in Europe, Asia, and Africa, as well as North America. The adult is dark brown with golden tints. Eagles' nests are called *aeries*. Bald eagles usually build their aeries in tall trees, near water. Golden eagles prefer rock ledges.

Falcons look like streamlined hawks. They flap their wings more quickly than hawks. Their wings are also longer and more pointed than hawks' and their tails are longer. *Gyrfalcons* are the largest falcons. They live in the Arctic and eat rodents and smaller birds. *Sparrow hawks* are small North American falcons. They perch on telephone poles and trees, then race off after flying insects they spot with their sharp eyes. The *duck hawk*, or *peregrine falcon*, swoops down on its prey at 225 miles an hour (362 km/hr)! Ducks, geese, and other birds are its favorite prey.

Hunters and Fishers   The *secretary bird* of Africa is the only member of its family, which means that no other birds are classified with it. The secretary bird, with gray and black plumage, has a long neck and long legs. It is about 4 feet (1.2 m) tall. It is the only bird of prey that hunts on foot. Secretary birds kill harmful insects and snakes.

One bird-of-prey family includes all kites, hawks, eagles, and Old World vultures. Kites are found all over the world. Four kinds live in North America. Kites have long, narrow wings. Do you remember what that means? Kites hunt in the air. *Mississippi* and *white-tailed kites* look much like falcons. Black and purple *swallow-tailed kites* have forked tails. The broad-winged *Everglades kites* are almost extinct. Kites do not dive headfirst at their prey. They swoop downward feet first and grab with their powerful claws.

Male hawks are usually smaller than females. Males range from 10 to 22 inches (25 to 56 cm) long. Their wings are broader than a falcon's and a little bit rounder. Hawks are strong fliers and have excellent eyesight. Hawks eat all of their prey, including the bones and fur or feathers. They vomit balls, or *pellets*, of the portions they cannot digest.

North American hawks are divided into two large groups, bird hawks and buzzard hawks. *Buzzard hawks* have large bodies, broad, rounded wings, and broad tails. The *red-tailed*, *red-shouldered*, *white-tailed*, and *black* hawks are all buzzard hawks. Buzzard hawks soar overhead and dive at their prey. *Bird hawks* have long tails and short wings. They glide frequently. The *goshawk* is the largest of the bird hawks. *Sharp-shinned hawks* often prey on pigeons, birds as big as the hawks themselves. The *harrier hawks*, found in many parts of the world, have long, pointed wings. The only North American harrier is the *marsh hawk*, which swoops low over the ground as it hunts. *Ospreys*, or *fish hawks*, are found near water all over the world. They eat only fish. They fly high over the water, then dive on their prey. They sometimes go completely under water to catch a meal.

Carrion Eaters Vultures, also called *buzzards*, live in most warm parts of the world. They eat carrion. They soar high in the sky and can see dead animals from very great distances. Their heads are bald. Vultures build no nests. They hatch their young on the ground—on rock or in caves.

The *California condor* is the largest North American land bird. It can be more than 50 inches (1.25 m) long, and has a wingspread of 8 to 11 feet (2.4 to 3.3 m). These condors sometimes live 50 years. Females lay only one egg a year. California condors are almost extinct. The *turkey vultures* are very common and live almost everywhere in the U.S. They are about 30 inches (76 cm) long. They have black feathers and red heads. *Black vultures* live in the southern U.S. and Central and South America. They sometimes live in cities, where they feed on garbage. Old World vultures, such as the Egyptian vulture and the lammergeier, are also carrion eaters, but they are members of the hawk family.

ALSO READ: BIRD, BIRDS OF THE PAST, FALCONRY, OWL.

▶ *Three birds of the past. Birds probably evolved from reptiles, but little is known about the oldest birdlike creature,* Archaeopteryx.

BIRDS OF THE PAST The beautiful red cardinal singing in the maple tree does not look like the black garter snake crawling on the ground. But birds and reptiles are related. Both hatch from eggs. Both have skin without sweat glands. They have similar bone structures and digestive systems. But important changes occurred, which separated birds from reptiles.

The first evidence of birdlike creatures is thought to be about 150 million years ago. A *fossil* (the remains of an animal or plant) called *Archaeopteryx* was discovered in Germany in the 19th century. This ancient animal had a tail like that of a lizard, a jaw with teeth, and feathers. It was the size of a crow and could probably glide through the air from a high tree to a lower one. Its forelegs were more like hands than wings, and claws stuck out from the "wing" edge.

Fossils of birdlike creatures from the next 30 or 40 millions of years are missing. Birds' bones are not often fossilized because they are easily smashed. Then, fossils of two North American creatures show what was happening to birds. *Hesperornis regalis* probably lived 60 to 120 million years ago. It was about 6 feet (1.8 m) tall. It could not fly, but it could swim. It

Most birds of prey have very sharp eyesight. It has been said that a hawk's vision can be likened to that of a man using binoculars that show things eight times their size.

Hesperornis

Archaeopteryx

Ichthyornis

▲ *Otto von Bismarck, German statesman.*

The most abundant species of birds ever known was the passenger pigeon of North America. It has been estimated that there were over five billion of these birds, over one fourth of the total bird population of the United States. The entire species was wiped out during the 19th century. They were killed in their nesting areas, shipped to the cities, and sold at food markets for about two cents apiece. The last passenger pigeon died in the Zoological Gardens of Cincinnati, Ohio, in 1914.

had the beginnings of a beak. *Ichthyornis victor* was a flying bird that looked like a gull.

By 60 million years ago, birds were much like those of today. Light hollow beaks had replaced jaws with teeth by that time. The lizardlike tail had shortened. The claws had disappeared from the wings. The part of the brain that controls vision and flying had increased in size. Birds had become fast, skillful flyers because they had developed ridges on their breastbones, to which strong muscles could be attached.

After birds learned to fly, some of them lost the power and adapted to a ground or water existence. Other birds evolved into the great variety of birds living today. In the past 200 years, human destruction has caused many birds to become "birds of the past," or extinct. Passenger pigeons by the millions lived in the eastern half of the United States 100 years ago. They fed on acorns and beech-tree nuts. People cut down the beech trees and the oaks, and killed millions of these birds for food. The last passenger pigeon, who was named Martha, died in a zoo in 1914.

The dodo, a turkey-sized flightless bird of Mauritius Island in the Indian Ocean, was killed off in the 1600's. The Carolina parakeet was once numerous in the South. But it is extinct now because people wanted its colorful feathers. The great auk, Labrador duck, and Eskimo curlew are some other extinct birds, killed off by people. Over 50 other American species are in danger of becoming extinct.

ALSO READ: BIRD, EVOLUTION, FOSSIL, FLIGHTLESS BIRDS, REPTILE.

BIRTH CERTIFICATE An official form filled out whenever a baby is born in the United States and most other countries is called a birth certificate. It lists the date, place, and time of a child's birth and is filed with the

state or county health department. The names of the mother and father and the signature of the doctor who helped the mother give birth to the baby also appear on the birth certificate.

Your birth certificate can be very helpful when you grow up. It proves who you are, how old you are, and where you were born. These facts may be important in getting a job, marrying, traveling out of the country, or inheriting property.

Births have been recorded for hundreds of years in the parish records of Christian churches. These records, usually made at the time of the child's baptism, were the custom for hundreds of years before birth registration became a job of government. People looking for records of their ancestors most often seek out old church records.

ALSO READ: LAW, PASSPORTS AND VISAS.

BIRTHDAY see ANNIVERSARY.

BIRTHSTONE see GEM.

BISMARCK, OTTO VON (1815–1898) The man who gathered many small kingdoms into modern, powerful Germany was Otto von Bismarck. He was born in Prussia, now northern Germany. Bismarck studied law at the universities of Gottingen and Berlin. After serving in the Prussian legislature for 11 years, he became ambassador, first to Russia, then to France.

In 1862 he became prime minister of Prussia. Prussia was then one of 39 weak German states. Bismarck wanted to unite all the states into one strong nation. He organized 22 states into the North German Confederation, in 1867, with Prussia as leader.

To unite the rest of Germany, Bismarck steered Prussia into three wars. First, Prussia fought with Austria against Denmark. Then Prussia turned against and defeated Austria. Prussia's war with France, from 1870 to 1871, established the German Empire. The German states not in the confederation helped Prussia win, then found themselves part of the empire.

Wilhelm I became emperor. But Bismarck became chancellor (chief minister of state). He ruled for 19 years and made Germany a strong industrial power. He was called the "Iron Chancellor" because he allowed no one to disagree with him. He said that only "iron and blood" could unite Germany. In 1888, Wilhelm II became emperor. He was jealous of Bismarck's power, which he wanted for himself. So he forced Bismarck to retire in 1890.

ALSO READ: GERMAN HISTORY, GERMANY, WORLD WAR I.

BISON When people began to explore the American West, they marveled at the large, shaggy brown animals they saw running in great herds. These animals were bison, often called American buffaloes.

The bison is a hoofed animal with a humped back and long, coarse hair. The male bison, or bull, ranks as the biggest mammal in North America. It may be 10 feet (3 m) long and as much as 6 feet (1.8 m) tall at the shoulder. The female, or cow, is smaller, with a lighter brown coat. Both sexes have small, short horns that curve inward.

The start of the mating season is announced in late summer by loud bellowings, as bulls fight to choose their mates. A single calf is born to each mother the next spring. In a few days the young can run with the herd to search for grass.

American Indians once hunted bison for their meat, hides, horns,

hoofs, and sinews (tendons). White settlers and hunters then discovered the valuable animals. Fewer than 600 bison were left by 1899 because thousands of bison were slaughtered. Laws were passed to protect the remaining animals and slowly the herds became larger again—between 30,000 and 35,000 in both the United States and Canada. But they live only in protected areas. A cousin of the American bison is the *wisent* of Europe. It is now extinct in the wild, but about 400 live in the safety of zoos.

ALSO READ: BUFFALO, CATTLE, HOOFED ANIMAL, MAMMAL.

▲ *The American bison, or buffalo, once roamed the western prairies in vast herds. After being brought close to extinction by hunters, the bison now survives in the safety of game reserves.*

BLACK AMERICANS Did you know that one in every eight U.S. citizens has ancestors who came from Africa? Because the sunlight there is hot and bright, the distant ancestors of today's black Americans developed very dark skins. It is dark skin that helps to protect a person from any harmful effects of the sun's rays. The term Negroes, which comes from the Spanish word for black, was used to describe black Americans, as well as blacks in Africa.

Black History What sort of land did the ancestors of black Americans live

BLACK AMERICANS

▼ *A black couple who lived in the Congo region of Africa at the time the first white explorers arrived.*

From the year 1808 no slaves could be brought into the United States. But in 1860 there were still almost 4 milion black slaves working in the country, nearly one-third of the total population of the Southern states.

in? Imagine that you are on a sightseeing tour of ancient Meroë, the capital city of Kush in the Sudan region of East Africa. The time is about 300 B.C., and this great empire is at its height. As you go through the city, you see many fascinating things. The soldiers' spears are made of iron, and so are many other tools. You notice hundreds of furnaces where the iron is smelted.

There are large stone buildings and great pyramids that look much like the pyramids of Egypt. You pass a temple lined with huge columns, and you notice the writing on the temple walls. A black nobleman rides past you on an elephant. Black traders in the busy marketplace tell you that they travel to Arabia, Greece, India, and even to China. They show you the cloth, jewels, and spices they have brought back. You see beautiful sculpture and painted pottery.

Have you ever heard of Kush? This nation was the oldest civilization of ancient Africa. But Kush was not the only mighty empire of ancient Africa. Some of the greatest of the African civilizations were the empires of Ghana, Mali, and Songhai in western Africa, all of which had strong armies and well-organized governments. These empires—and others—contributed to the languages, customs, traditions, and arts and crafts of the black peoples. But many black people of Africa were forced to take up another way of life.

In the 1400's, Portuguese explorers arrived on the African continent. They took black Africans back to Europe as servants. When Christopher Columbus reached America, blacks were with him. Pecho Alonso Niño, one of Columbus's sailors, is believed to have been a black. Other black people traveled and worked with the Spanish explorers in South and Central America. Estevanico ("Little Steven") explored northern Mexico and much of what are now the states of Arizona and New Mexico.

When French priests explored Canada, black people were with them, too. Blacks helped build the trading posts that became the cities of St. Louis, Missouri, and New Orleans, Louisiana. Another black person, Jean DuSable, built a trading post in 1779. The city of Chicago now stands at this spot.

Slavery in America Slavery is at least as old as written history. Slaves were usually prisoners taken in war. Sometimes they were criminals. They were forced to do the hard work of pulling the oars in ancient ships, of mining, or of farming. But slaves were usually permitted to marry, to own property, and even to buy their freedom.

When the New World was discovered, Europeans dreamed of great wealth and power. To make their dreams real, white people needed cheap labor. They soon thought of the blacks, who were considered "different" from them. Blacks looked different, spoke different languages, and were not Christians. These differences made it easier for Europeans to pretend that Africans could not rule themselves, and that it was right for the white people to take over.

The first black slaves arrived in the Spanish colonies of South America in 1501. But they could buy their freedom, and if they became Christians, they were set free.

In the English colonies of North America, heavy work was done not by slaves, but by *indentured servants*. These people agreed to work for a certain number of years (usually seven or ten) in return for a free trip to America. At the end of the time, the servants became free.

The first indentured servants were English people. Then, in 1619, the first black "servants" were brought to Jamestown, Virginia. These people were treated just as any other indentured servants. But this changed quickly. The planters of the colonies always had trouble finding workers. Colonists tried using Indians as workers, but the Indians disappeared into the forests. White indentured servants could easily run away to another colony, where no one could know that they had been servants. When the white servants completed their period of labor, the planters had to find new workers.

Colonists soon realized two things —blacks could not run away (their "different" skin color could not be hidden), and they were not Christians. So planters soon began to demand laws that would make slaves of black servants. Virginia passed such a law in 1669. The law stated that black servants were slaves for life, and so were their children. Another law said that even if a black became a Christian, he or she would still be a slave. By 1749, all 13 colonies had similar laws. The black was no longer a person but was a "thing," just like a chair or table! There were even laws that said that masters could not be accused of murdering their slaves—people would not destroy their own "property" on purpose!

Southern colonists discovered that three crops—rice, tobacco, and cotton—grew well on their land. All three of these crops require much land and many workers. The plantations demanded more slaves.

The colonists tried to believe that black people were contented with their lives as slaves. But black men, women, and children were no more "suited" to slavery than any other people. The lives of the slaves were usually horrible. Slaves had good food and clothing only if their masters gave them these things. Slaves were not allowed to learn to read or write. Slaves could be beaten. They could be sold, never to see their families again. They could even be killed—on the whim of their masters.

The law gave blacks no rights, so they did the only things they could— they fought or they tried to escape.

Blacks attacked the crews of the ships that carried them to America. Many captives refused to eat and starved themselves to death. Many others drowned themselves. Once in America, many blacks fought against the bonds of slavery. Slaves revolted against their owners. About two hundred slave revolts occurred in the United States alone.

Blacks sometimes fought on the same side as whites, not against them. Blacks fought in the American Revolution and in every American war since. Black soldiers of the American Revolution include Deborah Gannett, who—disguised as a man—fought the British for 18 months and won a medal for her heroism; Salem Poor, who fought in the battle of Bunker Hill; Peter Salem, who killed the British commander at the Battle of Bunker Hill, Boston; and Crispus Attucks, who was killed earlier during the Boston Massacre. But when the American Revolution was over, these brave soldiers were quickly forgotten. Once again, blacks were thought of only as slaves.

By the time the Civil War broke out 15 of the states had slaves, and 18 had no slavery. The Civil War produced many black heroes and heroines. For example, before the fighting began, Harriet Tubman escaped from slavery in the South and returned many times to lead more than 300

▲ *During the time that slavery existed in the United States, many black families were cruelly split up and sold at auction.*

▼ *Blacks in other countries were often conquered by white empire-builders. This is Queen Ranavallo III of Madagascar. The French took over this black island kingdom in 1896, and the queen was forced to leave the country.*

There are more than 28 million black American citizens. Two and a half million of them are in New York State.

▼ *Black African culture is rich and varied. The Hausa of Nigeria, seen here in their flowing robes, are a black people of West Africa.*

other slaves to freedom. She also worked as a nurse for the Union Army during the war.

After the Civil War ended in 1865, the Thirteenth Amendment to the Constitution was passed, and slavery was declared illegal in the United States. For the first time, blacks in the United States were regarded as free people by the Constitution. But the fight for equality was far from over.

Picking Up the Pieces The South was in ruins at the end of the Civil War. Fields were covered with weeds, houses were wrecked, families were separated. The freed blacks had no jobs and no money. They did not trust the whites and the whites did not trust them.

Southern whites soon took control of state governments. They passed local laws meant to keep blacks from being treated as their equals. Black people were not allowed to travel freely or to testify in court against white people. Other laws stated that blacks without jobs would be arrested and fined. Those who could not pay the fine would be forced to work for someone who would pay it. Many blacks were effectively made slaves again.

Congress passed a law giving the Union Army control of the southern state governments, and most of the unfair southern laws were overturned. This was the period known as *Reconstruction* (rebuilding), which lasted 12 years from 1865 to 1877. During this time, many blacks were elected to public office. Robert Smalls, who captured the Confederate ship *Planter* and later commanded it for the Union, was elected to Congress, as was Francis Cardozo. Blanche Bruce served in the U.S. Senate, as did Hiram R. Revels. Pinckney B. S. Pinchback became governor of Louisiana and was elected to the U.S. Senate in 1873. White senators said he was not "coopera-

tive," and they refused to let him take his place.

Many other blacks served in state legislatures. Most of them were good, honest people who worked hard. But a few were dishonest. Some white Southerners were quick to point this out. The North grew tired of spending time and money on the South. Black leaders were voted out of office, one by one. By 1877, Union troops were gone from the South, whites controlled the governments, and Reconstruction was finished.

Black Leaders When Reconstruction was over, southern governments again passed laws that practically made black people slaves. Blacks had to ride in separate railroad cars, use separate drinking fountains, and attend separate schools. They were restricted from voting by various laws, and secret societies such as the Ku Klux Klan terrorized blacks and discouraged them from exercising their rights. The Klan was founded in 1866 and, though suppressed, has reappeared several times, especially in the 1960's. Congress ended most voting restrictions when it passed the Voting Rights Act in 1965.

But even in the 1870's, some things *were* different. Then the blacks had newspapers and schools, and they could keep in touch with one another. The blacks also had leaders. One leader was Booker T. Washington. He believed that the black people needed training before they could build buildings, manage factories, and grow crops. He was afraid that blacks would move too quickly in making the change from slavery to freedom, bringing about more problems than successes. Many blacks supported Washington's ideas, as did many whites.

Other black leaders disagreed with Washington. One of the most important black leaders of the early 1900's was W. E. B. Du Bois, who was born in Massachusetts, the son of a successful lawyer. Du Bois said blacks were not moving fast enough. He demanded immediate full and equal rights for all blacks.

In 1909, Du Bois and many other black leaders joined with a group of white people to form the National Association for the Advancement of Colored People (NAACP). This organization has won many legal battles that have helped to give black people the rights they were guaranteed in the Thirteenth Amendment.

Two other black groups were formed at about the same time. The Urban League's purpose was to help black people adjust to living in large northern cities. The Universal Negro Improvement Association was led by Marcus Garvey. Garvey was the first person to use the saying, "Black is beautiful." He said that blacks should not try to "fit into" the United States. He wanted black people to return to Africa.

Blacks Today Blacks have had to fight for rights that whites of European ancestry have been able to assume from birth. They have gained many of those rights, particularly in the years since the 1960's, but the struggle is still going on.

Black people have entered many occupations that were once closed to them. Colleges and universities admit blacks, and often provide scholarships for those who cannot afford tuition. The numbers of blacks in such institutions has increased by more than 50 per cent since 1970.

Blacks work as doctors, lawyers, teachers, engineers, and scientists, and serve in federal and state legislatures and other elective offices. Some have served as ambassadors. For example, Andrew Young was U.S. ambassador to the United Nations from 1977 to 1979 and was succeeded by another black, Donald F. McHenry, while Patricia Roberts Harris was ambassador to Luxembourg, 1965–1967. She later became the first black

▲ *Dr. Martin Luther King, Jr. (left) received the 1964 Nobel Peace Prize for his nonviolent leadership of the U.S. civil rights movement.*

woman in the Cabinet when President Jimmy Carter appointed her Secretary of Housing and Urban development. In the 1984 and 1988 presidential campaigns, the Rev. Jesse Jackson, a Baptist minister, made a strong bid to run as the Democratic candidate.

Jackson had already made a name for himself as a black civil rights leader. In 1971 he founded Operation PUSH, which stands for People United to Serve Humanity. It is one of many organizations through which blacks are still fighting for complete equality with whites.

Some of these organizations, such as the NAACP, work through the courts. In one legal case in 1954, the Supreme Court said that segregated schools (separate schools for black children and white children) are illegal because "separate" cannot be "equal." Other organizations, such as the Southern Christian Leadership Conference (which was led by Martin Luther King until he was murdered in 1968), have used marches and nonviolent demonstrations to bring about changes. Some groups, such as the Black Muslims, have stressed independence and have established separate, black- owned businesses, stores, farms, and schools.

Some black people are militant and believe that only through force can

▼ *Jesse Owens, a black sports hero of the 1930's, earned worldwide praise for his athletic feats.*

▲ *Blacks excel in many sports. There have been many famous black track and field champions, such as sprint star Evelyn Ashford.*

▼ *Black presidential candidate Jesse Jackson is a widely respected political figure.*

blacks achieve equality. This is frightening to many black and white people. However, through education and books, such as Alex Haley's *Roots*, blacks have become deeply aware of their African and American ancestry. Today, they know what they are legally entitled to as citizens.

For further information on:

African Black History, *see* AFRICA, ANCIENT CIVILIZATIONS, SLAVERY.

Black People in the Arts, *see* ANDERSON, MARIAN; ARMSTRONG, LOUIS; BALDWIN, JAMES; BROOKS, GWENDOLYN; HANDY, W. C.; HUGHES, JAMES LANGSTON; JACKSON, MAHALIA; WRIGHT, RICHARD.

Black People in Government, *see* BROOKE, EDWARD; BRUCE, BLANCHE K.; BUNCHE, RALPH; HARRIS, PATRICIA; MARSHALL, THURGOOD; YOUNG, ANDREW.

Black People in Science, *see* CARVER, GEORGE WASHINGTON.

Black People in Sports, *see* GIBSON, ALTHEA; LOUIS, JOE; OWENS, JESSE; ROBINSON, JACKIE.

Black People in Education, *see* BETHUNE, MARY MCLEOD; WASHINGTON, BOOKER T.

Black History During the Eighteenth Century, *see* AMERICAN COLONIES; AMERICAN REVOLUTION; BANNEKER, BENJAMIN.

Black History During the Nineteenth Century, *see* ABOLITION; CIVIL WAR; CONFEDERATE STATES OF AMERICA; DOUGLASS, FREDERICK; EMANCIPATION PROCLAMATION; RECONSTRUCTION; TRUTH, SOJOURNER; TUBMAN, HARRIET; TURNER, NAT; UNDERGROUND RAILROAD; WASHINGTON, BOOKER T.

Black History During the Twentieth Century, *see* BLACK MUSLIMS; CIVIL RIGHTS; CIVIL RIGHTS MOVEMENT; DAVIS, BENJAMIN OLIVER; KING, MARTIN LUTHER, JR.; MALCOLM X; NATIONAL ASSOCIATION FOR THE ADVANCEMENT OF COLORED PEOPLE; NATIONAL URBAN LEAGUE; YOUNG, WHITNEY.

BLACKFOOT INDIANS Restless Indians wandered the plains of Montana and lower Canada, following the bison (American buffalo) herds. The bison was vital to the life of the Blackfoot. They ate its meat and made colorful tepees from buffalo hides. They also made warm robes, cooking vessels, saddles, and moccasins. They dyed their moccasins black, which may have given the tribe its name.

The Blackfoot were Plains Indians and their language belonged to the Algonkian language family. The Plains Indians hunted in various ways. Some Blackfoot Indians would drive a herd of bison over a cliff so that there were meat and hides for all.

When Spanish explorers brought horses to America, the Blackfoot learned to hunt bison on horseback. But in the 19th century, the bison disappeared from the plains and so did the Blackfoot way of life. Today these Indians are farmers.

ALSO READ: ALGONKIAN; INDIANS, AMERICAN.

BLACK HOLE When a large star dies it does so as a *supernova*—an unbelievably violent explosion. Afterwards, all that is left is a shroud of gas moving outward from a squashed-in central remnant. This remnant may be a *pulsar* (small heavenly body giving out radio pulses at regular intervals), but for a very large star it will be a black hole.

A black hole is quite frightening; in a way it is not really there! All of its matter is crushed right out of existence. But the black hole has the same gravity as if its matter were still present but compressed (squashed) into a very small volume. In fact, the gravity is so intense that not even light can escape it. That is why black holes are "black." Anything else that goes into a black hole is also crushed out of existence at the hole's central point, or *singularity.* So black holes are like cosmic "vacuum cleaners," sucking up dust and other stars.

It is likely that when the universe came into being with the "Big Bang" thought most likely by scientists, billions of *mini black holes*, about the size of an atom, were created by that terrific explosion. At the heart of most galaxies may be a *super black hole*, perhaps millions of times more massive than our sun.

Our universe, billions of years from now, may finish as a vast black hole.

ALSO READ: ATOM, GALAXY, GRAVITY AND GRAVITATION, STAR, UNIVERSE.

BLACK MUSLIMS Black Muslims are members of a social and religious movement. The religion's official name is the *Nation of Islam.* It is based on the faith of Islam, and teaches blacks to be proud of being black. Members want blacks to be economically separate from white people and even to have their own all-black lands in America.

Black Muslims adopt Arabic names, or use their own first name with an X as a last name. The X stands for the African name the ancestors of the Black Muslims lost when they were forced into slavery. Faithful members must be thrifty and clean. They cannot use alcoholic beverages, drugs, or tobacco. Each member gives one-tenth of his earnings to the Nation of Islam.

The movement began in Detroit, Michigan, in 1930. Its founder was Wali Farad, born Wallace D. Fard. When Farad disappeared in 1934, Elijah Muhammad (born Elijah Poole in 1897) became leader. Elijah's son Wallace took control following the death of his father in 1975.

Malcolm X (born Malcolm Little in 1925) was a chief spokesman for them in the early 1960's. He formed a rival group in 1964 and was assassinated in 1965. This caused great turmoil among the Black Muslims, but later calm was restored.

ALSO READ: BLACK AMERICANS, CIVIL RIGHTS MOVEMENT, ISLAM, MALCOLM X, MUHAMMAD, RELIGION.

BLACK SEA The Black Sea would be a lake if it were not for its narrow passage through the Turkish Straits (Bosporus and Dardanelles) into the Aegean Sea and the Mediterranean beyond. The sea was probably named "black" because of the heavy fogs that make the waters look very dark during winter.

The Soviet Union's only warm-water ports, such as Odessa, lie on the Black Sea. Bulgaria, Romania, and Turkey also have ports on this sea. (See the map with the article on EUROPE.) Soviet naval ships and cargo ships from several lands sail across the Black Sea and through the Bosporus, the Sea of Marmara, and the Dardanelles Sea into the Mediterranean. Whatever nation has controlled the Bosporus and the Dardanelles in the past, has controlled traffic going in and out of the Black Sea. Turkey, the "doorkeeper" of this crossroads of commerce today, permits the passage of the Soviet ships.

Several rivers drain into the Black Sea. The most important, the Danube, flows through central and eastern Europe. Three major Soviet rivers flow into the Black Sea—the Dnieper, Dniester, and Don.

Fishing boats come into Black Sea ports loaded with herring, mackerel, pike, and sturgeon. Coal is shipped out of Turkish ports on the south coast. Tropical fruits, tea, and cotton are raised along the hot, humid, northern coast. Soviet workers go for free winter vacations at resorts along these warm, sunny shores.

ALSO READ: BULGARIA, DANUBE RIVER, ROMANIA, SOVIET UNION, TURKEY.

▲ *Elijah Muhammad, spiritual leader of the Black Muslims in the United States until his death in 1975.*

▲ *Elizabeth Blackwell, first woman doctor in the United States.*

BLACKWELL, ELIZABETH

(1821–1910) Elizabeth Blackwell was born in England and grew up in America. She decided to be a doctor, but no woman had ever been one before. Many doctors did not believe a woman should do their work. Eight colleges turned her down. Then, the Geneva (New York) College of Medicine bravely accepted her as a student, and she became a doctor in 1849. Five years later, her younger sister, Emily, also became a doctor.

Dr. Blackwell wanted to be a surgeon, but had to give up when she went blind in one eye. She went to Paris, France, but hospitals would let her do only students' work. She returned to America.

Dr. Blackwell could not get a job, although she was trained and talented. Finally, with Emily and a young Polish woman doctor, she started a clinic for poor people in New York, called the New York Infirmary. Dr. Blackwell later opened the first women's medical college in America. She helped train many nurses during the Civil War.

She later returned to England, where she helped open the London School of Medicine for Women. In England, too, Dr. Blackwell was the first woman to ever practice medicine.

ALSO READ: MEDICINE.

BLEACHING

The procedure for whitening cloth, paper, or any material is called bleaching. Most bleaching is done with chemicals. These are often very strong and can burn the skin, if used carelessly.

Chlorine bleach is good for whitening cotton and linen. It is made from chloride of lime dissolved in water. Soaking material in the bleach removes the color from the threads or fibers, so that it dries white. Another good bleaching agent is hydrogen peroxide. Some people use hydrogen peroxide to turn their hair blond. Silk and wool are bleached by wetting them and exposing them to the gas sulfur dioxide. Sulfur dioxide is the gas you smell when a match has just been lit. More than 3,000 years ago, the Egyptians and Babylonians bleached by spreading wet cloth on a surface exposed to the rays of the sun.

■ LEARN BY DOING

You can try sun bleaching too. You will need two sheets of construction paper, one blue and one yellow. Cut the yellow paper into a smaller square, and lay it on the center of the blue sheet. Put the sheets of paper into a sunny window for about ten days. Lift off the yellow sheet. What do you see? Try cutting designs in yellow paper and bleaching a blue picture. ■

ALSO READ: TEXTILE.

BLIMP   see AIRSHIP.

BLIND, EDUCATION OF THE
see SPECIAL EDUCATION.

BLINDFISH   Most of the fish that you are familiar with have eyes. However, some fish live in places where eyes are not needed. Fish that live in caves or deep oceans where light cannot reach do not need eyes. These fish are called *blindfish*. Though they do not have eyes, blindfish have tiny organs on their heads and bodies that give them a keen sense of touch.

The most common kind of blindfish live in the waters of caves in eastern United States and Europe.

Blindfish are usually less than 5 inches (12.7 cm) long and have a light pink color. Their blood shows through the flesh, causing the pink body color.

BLINDNESS   see SIGHT.

Some foods are bleached. Sugar and flour, for example, are bleached white to make them more attractive for the market. Other things bleached are paper, feathers, hair, and ivory.

BLOOD   Blood has been called the "river of life." It could also be called "the living river." About half of the total amount of blood in the human body is made of living cells that take food and oxygen to the tissues of the body and carry off waste products. The other half is a yellowish liquid called *plasma*. Blood substances also fight germs that can cause disease.

The heart pumps blood through the body. Blood flows from the heart to the lungs, where it gives up a waste product, the gas carbon dioxide, that it has collected from the body. This gas is breathed out, and, in exchange, the blood picks up fresh oxygen. Blood then returns to the heart, which pumps it through the arteries to the whole body. Along the way, the blood delivers oxygen to all the cells of the body and collects carbon dioxide from the cells. The blood returns to the heart through the veins.

Types of Cells   Blood has two types of cells—each with a different job. *Red cells* carry oxygen and carbon dioxide. *White cells* help fight infections. And small, colorless particles, called *platelets*, help in making blood clots.

The red cells are the most numerous, as well as the smallest cells in the blood. They are so small that 3,000 of them side by side would measure only one inch (2.5 cm). They pick up oxygen in the lungs and carry it to the cells of the body. They also bring back carbon dioxide to the lungs. Red cells are bright red when they carry oxygen. But they turn dark red when they lose their oxygen. Red cells work very hard and live only about three to four weeks. Red cells are made in the marrow of bones to replace those that are worn out. A body can make billions of new red cells every hour.

There is one white cell for about every 600 red cells in the blood. White cells fight disease-causing bacteria. They increase in number when there is an infection anywhere in the body. They surround the infected area and isolate it. The yellowy-white matter formed is called *pus*. Dead cells and germs are in the pus.

For about every 18 red cells there is one platelet. Platelets help in clotting the blood. When a blood vessel is cut, platelets gather and form a plug that helps to stop the bleeding. If blood did not clot, it would run out of even a small cut until the body was completely drained of blood.

Plasma is mostly water. But it also contains other substances, especially *proteins*. One type of protein helps platelets to make clots. Another contains antibodies that protect a person from diseases. Plasma also carries hormones, vitamins, enzymes, and minerals. The body needs all of these.

Blood Types   When a person loses a lot of blood, it can be replaced by blood from another person. This is a *transfusion*. A blood transfusion can save a life. But a person who gets a blood transfusion must have blood that is the same type as his own blood, or a type that will not harm his own.

There are four basic types of human blood, each with different substances in it. They were first identified by an Austrian doctor, Karl Landsteiner, in 1901. The types are called A, B, AB, and O. Type O can

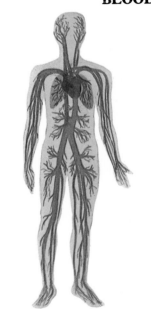

▲ *The network of arteries circulates blood around the body.*

▼ *A blood transfusion transfers blood from one person (the donor) to another. Here a donor is giving blood for storage in a blood bank.*

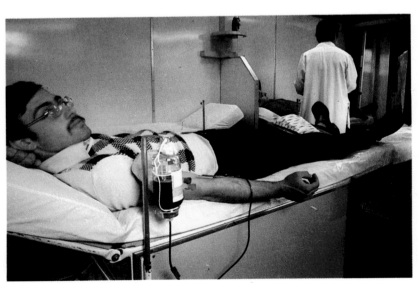

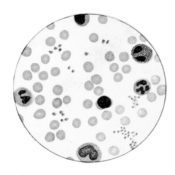

▲ *The make-up of normal blood. Red blood cells are the small pink shapes. White blood cells are the large red and brown shapes. Platelets are the small dots. These three parts of the blood float in the pale-yellow liquid called plasma.*

▼ *Coracles are skin boats that have been used for more than 8,000 years.*

be given to anyone. People with type O blood are called *universal donors*. People with type AB can usually receive all other types, so they are called *universal recipients*.

Blood can be transfused directly from one person to another. But most transfusions are given with blood that has been collected from donors and stored in a blood bank. So any type of blood is available when needed.

ALSO READ: ANTIGEN AND ANTIBODY, BONE, BREATHING, CIRCULATORY SYSTEM, HUMAN BODY, LYMPH, METABOLISM, PROTEIN.

BLUME, JUDY (born 1938) Problems are a part of growing up, and the stories Judy Blume writes describe teenage anxieties vividly.

Judy Blume was born at Elizabeth, New Jersey. She was graduated from New York University and married John M. Blume. They had two children, but the marriage ended in divorce.

The book that first brought Judy Blume fame was *Are You There, God? It's Me, Margaret* (1970). In it she tells of the worries of an 11-year-old girl over religion and the development of her body.

In a similar way she portrays in *It's Not the End of the World* (1973) the struggles of a young girl to stop her parents from seeking divorce, while *Blubber* (1974) describes the miseries of a girl who is overweight.

Judy Blume has also written books for adults, including *Smart Women* (1983).

ALSO READ: CHILDREN'S LITERATURE.

BLUSHING see SKIN.

BOATS AND BOATING Power boats race across the lake at 40 miles an hour (64 km/hr). Another open

boat chugs toward shallow fishing water. Houseboats carry happy families on floating vacations. Sleek sailboats skim back and forth in the breeze. Boats of all sizes, shapes, and colors attract people to America's waterways. More than 15 million Americans own some kind of boat today.

New Materials for Boats Most small boats were made of solid wood planks until the 1950's. The planks fit tightly together to form the *hull*, or bottom, of the boat. The most common boat before the 1950's was the simple rowboat. It was heavy and usually slow. Sometimes a rowboat was powered by a motor, usually outboard. But most of the time, its only power was the muscle of somebody using flat-bladed oars to move it through the water. Wooden-plank boats often leaked, especially if they were left out of the water for a long time. The wood shrank, leaving spaces between the planks. A standard springtime job was to fix leaks that developed during winter storage.

Fiberglass, aluminum, and steel replaced wood planks in modern boatbuilding. Fiberglass is a smooth,

▼ *Simple fishing boats, like these in Portugal, are used by fishermen along the seacoasts of the world.*

lightweight, plasticlike material with great strength. It can be molded, or formed, into any shape. Hulls of small boats can be made from one piece of fiberglass. Pre-shaped fiberglass sections are fastened together to make larger hulls. Aluminum makes good hulls for many small fishing boats, rowboats, and canoes. Aluminum boats weigh very little and are usually inexpensive. But because of their light weight, they bounce and rock more than other boats in rough water. For larger merchant vessels, steel is used because of its strength.

The newest boat-building material is cement. That sounds ridiculous—a cement boat would sink straight to the bottom. It would, except for one thing: this cement has more air bubbles than solid material. Wet cement is poured into a one-piece mold of the boat hull. Then millions of tiny air bubbles are blown into the cement, making a heavy foam that expands to fill the mold. After it dries, the cement boat hull is light enough to float. The cement makes a hull very strong. A cement hull is also strong because it has no seams or joints that can weaken.

A Shape for Every Need Weekend sailors can choose their boats from hundreds of different sizes, shapes, and prices. A sailboat offers adventure or relaxation, but it won't pull a water skier. A streamlined motorboat may be perfect for skiing or racing, but no good for deep-sea fishing. A large cruiser is a luxury floating holiday home, but it can't explore a narrow creek.

The most important feature of each kind of boat is the shape of the hull. Only two basic shapes are made, but there are many types of each. A *displacement hull* sits down low in the water. It pushes its way through the water. The water pushes back with great resistance, and this means the boat does not go very fast. But a boat with a displacement hull is stable in

rough water. A *planing hull* is V-shaped and rises in the water as the boat goes faster. A planing-hull boat moving quickly seems almost to skim along on top of the water. This lessens the water resistance and allows the boat to reach higher top speeds. But a planing hull is less stable than a displacement hull, so the boat must slow down in rough water.

A flat-bottom boat is one type of displacement hull. It is good for fishing in shallow water. Most family boats and all racing boats have planing hulls. As the motor goes faster, the *bow*, or front end, rises up out of the water, and the *stern*, or back end, sinks lower. Some newer boats, modeled after Polynesian outrigger craft, have two hulls (a *catamaran*) or even three (a *trimaran*). Catamarans and trimarans give higher speed without losing stability or safety.

Types of Boats in Use Today

CANOES. Canoes used to be made of wood, bark, or hide stretched over a frame. Today, canoes are usually made of fiberglass, aluminum, or other lightweight materials, rather than wood. In an open or Canadian-style canoe one person can sit in the bow and another person in the stern. Both people use paddles to propel the canoe along. The *kayak* is a closed canoe, with just a hole for the canoeist to sit in. Canoes are light and easy to carry. One or two adults, or three

▲ *A Peruvian reed boat on Lake Titicaca. Boats like this were used by the Inca ancestors of today's Peruvians.*

▼ *Wouldn't it be fun to live on a boat? Some people do. A floating home, or houseboat, may be moored at a permanent berth. Or it may have an engine and move about, whenever its owners feel like a change of scene.*

▲ *A barge is a flat-bottomed boat used on canals and rivers to carry freight. Some barges have their own engines, but others are towed by tugboats.*

▼ *Many people enjoy sailing. Most yachts have a fore-and-aft sail arrangement. The mainsail is the boat's chief sail, but when there is a following wind, a big, billowing spinnaker sail may be set too, as shown here.*

children, can carry (or *portage*) one from one stream to another. Canoes tip easily, and only good swimmers should use them. In rough waters, even a strong swimmer should wear a life jacket.

ROWBOATS. Rowboats are for fishing or just for drifting on a pond or lake. They are still often made of wood, although many are made of various plastics. The rowboat is propelled by one person seated in the middle of the boat. The rower can move the boat in any direction with two long-handled oars.

MOTORBOATS. The simplest form of motorboats is a rowboat with an outboard motor attached to the stern. The motor can be turned from side to side, and the pilot steers the boat in this way. Small motorboats are also called *speedboats* because they can travel 40 miles an hour (64 km/h) or more. Racing boats, called *hydroplanes* or *powerboats*, zoom along at over 100 miles an hour (160 km/hr), shooting out a huge spray or "rooster tail" behind. Powerboats compete in races, and also pull water skiers. Some motorboats are entirely open, others are partly closed. Many larger powered boats have inboard motors, housed inside the hull.

CABIN CRUISERS. Cabin cruisers are larger, fancier versions of motorboats. They can be up to 60 feet (18.2 m) long. Cruisers have enclosed cabins with *bunks* (beds) for two to ten or more people. They also house *galleys* (kitchens) and *heads* (toilets). Larger cabin cruisers are equipped with radar, ship-to-shore radiotelephones, and lifeboats. These large boats are oceangoing.

HOUSEBOATS. Like cabin cruisers, houseboats can often be classed as ships. These floating homes offer the comfort of land houses plus the fun of being on a boat. A houseboat owner bored with the location of his house starts the motor and pilots his home to a new place. Houseboats cruise slowly and smoothly because they

have flat-bottomed displacement hulls.

WORK BOATS. Tugboats, fireboats, and fishing boats are the most common work boats. Tugboats tow large ships in and out of harbors. Large ships have engines too powerful to use near docks, and the ships are so long that they are clumsy. So tugboats guide them to their berths and out again. Tugboats also haul loads of garbage, coal, sand, and other materials along many rivers. Tugboats are very stable and are often used to rescue sailors stranded in storms.

Fireboats are the fire engines of rivers and harbors, and many sailors trapped on burning ships owe their lives to these "floating firefighters."

Fishing boats come in many sizes and shapes. Some go far out to sea and others stay near the shore. Very modern fishing boats are equipped with radar and sonar devices that help them locate shoals of fish.

Many other work boats travel the waters of the world. Some cities, such as Venice, Italy, have canals instead of streets, and small boats (called *gondolas* in Venice) replace automobiles. The sampans and junks of Asia are cargo boats, floating restaurants, taxis, and even hotels. And ferry boats carry people—and animals, cars, and trucks—across rivers.

Safe Boating Everyone who rides in a boat should learn and use the simple rules of boating safety. Always make sure that each person wears a life jacket. Watch for swimmers, as well as for other boats, and don't cut too close to them. Don't speed past little boats or boats that are stopped for fishing or swimming. Head for shore if the weather looks as if it might turn bad. Carry lights for boating at night. The Coast Guard, which has a station in almost every large city, gives classes in boating safety.

ALSO READ: SAILING, SHIPS AND SHIPPING, WATER SKIING.

BODY SCANNER The body scanner is a new method of medical examination that allows very detailed pictures to be taken of the inside of the body. It uses *X rays* to photograph the internal organs, but unlike the ordinary X-ray picture, the body scanner produces pictures like a slice through part or all of the body.

The scanner is a large machine that moves over the patient being examined, then rotates very slowly, taking pictures as it travels around the patient in a circle. The "picture" is not made on X-ray film. Instead, the X rays passing through the patient are measured, and the readings obtained are fed to a computer. This puts together all the separate X-ray readings and turns them into a picture of the "slice" through the body, which appears on a TV screen. The picture can be colored by the computer to highlight body parts. An even newer type of body scanner does not use X rays. Instead, the patient is surrounded by huge magnets and machines for sending harmless radio waves through the body. With this scanner there is no danger from X rays, and the computer pictures are often better than those from X-ray scanners.

ALSO READ: X RAYS.

BOER WAR The Boers were European settlers of the land now called the Republic of South Africa. They fought for, and lost, some of their land in the Boer War, which was fought from 1899 to 1902.

Dutch settlers first reached the southern tip of Africa in 1652. Protestant religious refugees called *Huguenots* arrived from France to join the Dutch in 1688. These and other settlers, called *Boers* (the Dutch word for "farmers"), claimed more and more farmland during the next 100 years. In 1835 they began to move north, where they established the areas

▲ *The boats used for rowing races are lightweight, thin-hulled shells. Here a pair of double scullers put all their effort into a race.*

called the Orange Free State, Transvaal, and Natal as the Boer republic.

Diamonds were discovered in the Orange Free State in 1867. Fortune hunters came from all over the world, and the British seized the Transvaal in 1877 after gold was discovered there. But a two-year war there brought Boer independence in 1881. Miners struck gold at Witwatersrand five years later. British *Uitlanders* (foreigners) began coming into the country again. They settled down, but were not allowed by the Boer government to vote.

"Jameson's raiders," a group of British Uitlanders, tried to take over Johannesburg, the capital of Transvaal, in 1895. They failed, but British troops were gathering along the Transvaal border in support of the British settlers. Transvaal and the Orange Free State declared war on Great Britain.

The Boers, well equipped by Germany, won many victories during the early stages of the war. But the tide turned in 1900. New British troops led by Lord Roberts and Lord Kitchener soon captured the major Boer cities. The Boers, however, fled to the hills and began a guerrilla war under the leadership of Generals Botha and Smuts. The British put Boer women and children in prison camps and

Every Boy Scout of America knows the name Baden-Powell. Robert Baden-Powell was in command of the town of Mafeking throughout its 217-day siege by the Boers during the Boer War. When the long siege was lifted, Baden-Powell returned to England a hero. In 1910 he retired from the army and devoted the rest of his life to the Scout movement.

began combing the guerrilla country, section by section. On May 31, 1902, a peace treaty was signed at Pretoria. Transvaal and the Orange Free State became British colonies. Although the Boer leaders were not punished, the war left much bitterness.

ALSO READ: SOUTH AFRICA.

BOHEMIA   see CZECHOSLOVAKIA.

BOHR, NIELS HENRIK DAVID (1885–1962) The Danish scientist Niels Bohr was one of the great figures in the development of modern physics. He was also a great humanitarian. He received the 1922 Nobel Prize for physics, but later donated the gold medal to Finnish war relief.

Born in Denmark, he worked in British universities for some years before returning home in 1916 as Professor of Physics at Copenhagen University. There he worked out a new theory of the atom.

Bohr's theory was based on the idea that atoms consist of negatively charged electrons spinning around a positively charged nucleus. He said that as long as the electrons travel in fixed paths around the center of the atom, no energy is radiated—no light is given out. But when an electron "jumps" to an orbit closer to the center of the atom, it loses energy. This energy appears as a tiny "packet" of light that travels outward from the atom.

Scientists were puzzled by the particles inside the atom. Were they really particles, or were they just waves of energy? Bohr decided that our usual ways of picturing things do not work inside the tiny world of the atom. He said that the particle picture and the wave picture can both be right in certain circumstances.

ALSO READ: ATOM; ELEMENT; LIGHT; PLANCK, MAX; QUANTUM THEORY; SPECTRUM.

▲ *Simón Bolívar, liberator of South America.*

BOLEYN, ANNE   see HENRY, KINGS OF ENGLAND

BOLÍVAR, SIMÓN (1783–1830) One of South America's greatest statesmen and generals was Simón Bolívar. Called "The Liberator," he led the fight for independence from Spain.

Bolívar was born in Caracas, Venezuela, at a time when the American colonies to the north had just won independence from Britain. His family had lived in Venezuela for more than 200 years. Its first members arrived with Spanish settlers in the early 1500's. Bolívar's parents died when he was very young and left him a large fortune. He was able to travel widely in the United States and Europe and saw how revolutions were bringing new freedom.

When he was 28, Bolívar joined the fight for the freedom of Venezuela and all of South America from Spain. After a long struggle, he and his troops defeated the Spaniards in 1819, at the Battle of Boyaca (in Colombia). He became President of Greater Colombia (now Colombia, Venezuela, Panama and Ecuador). His army defeated the Spaniards at Ayacucho (in Peru). Upper Peru became Bolivia, named after Bolívar, who wrote the new state's constitution.

He hoped to form a united Spanish America, but many people hated him because of his dictatorial ways. Revolts occurred in many places. Bolívar barely escaped assassination in 1828. Greater Colombia split apart, and Bolívar resigned the presidency. He died of tuberculosis at age 47.

ALSO READ: BOLIVIA, VENEZUELA.

BOLIVIA The large country of Bolivia lies high in the Andes Mountains of South America. It has towering,

BOLIVIA

Capital City: La Paz, seat of government (955,000 people) and Sucre, legal capital (85,000 people).
Area: 424,164 square miles (1,098,581 sq. km).
Population: 6,870,000.
Government: Republic.
Natural Resources: Ranchland, forests, minerals.
Export Products: Natural gas, tin, coffee, sugar.
Unit of Money: Boliviano.
Official Language: Spanish.

snow-covered mountains; a high, windy plateau; and no seacoast. Brazil lies to the north and east. Paraguay and Argentina are to the south, and to the west are Chile and Peru. (See the map with the article on SOUTH AMERICA.)

Bolivia is nearly as large as Texas and California combined, but it has very few people. You can travel for a day in some areas without seeing a house. More than half the Bolivians are Quechua and Aymara Indians. About two-thirds of all Bolivians live on the *altiplano*, or "high plain." The altiplano lies more than 2 miles (3.2 km) above sea level, between two ranges of the Andes. The Indians have their own language. Most speak Aymara or Quechua and live much as they did before the Spanish conquered Bolivia in the 1500's. Some Indians make silver jewelry, pottery, and woven cloth. Indian herdsmen raise llamas, alpacas, and vicunas, and use their wool for clothing. Many Bolivians make their living by farming. The most important national industry, however, is mining. There are rich tin deposits in the Andes, though in the mid 1980's, the mining industry was in poor shape.

Most of Bolivia's cities are on the altiplano. La Paz is the highest capital in the world, at 12,795 feet (3,900 m) above sea level. Lake Titicaca, where fishermen sail light balsa-wood boats, is the world's highest lake, at 12,507 feet (3,812 m) above sea level.

Spanish conquistadors (conquerors) arrived in what is now Bolivia in 1538. They took away a fortune in Bolivian silver. Spain controlled Bolivia for nearly 300 years. A famous general, Simón Bolívar, helped form an independent government in 1825. The new nation was later named after him. Bolivia was named a republic and had its first constitution in 1826. Bolivia fought wars with Peru (1879–1883) and Paraguay (1930–1935). Through the years, powerful groups have seized control of the government. The leaders have sometimes ruled without paying attention to the laws or the Bolivian congress. Economic problems, labor strikes, and student protests have added to the country's continual troubles.

ALSO READ: SOUTH AMERICA.

BOMB see EXPLOSIVES.

BOMBAY On a large monument in the center of Bombay are the words, "Gateway to India." The city is built on an island in the Arabian Sea. Roads connect Bombay to the mainland. Its has a superb harbor.

Bombay is the capital of the Indian state of Maharashtra. The city has over eight million people. It is a melting pot for many different peoples. Most Bombay citizens are a Hindu people, the Mahrattas. The Parsees

▲ *Bolivia's government meets at La Paz. Founded in 1548, the city is the highest seat of government of any country in the world.*

▼ *Bombay's impressive Gateway to India arch was built in 1911. Its architecture is in the Indian Gujarat style of the 1500's.*

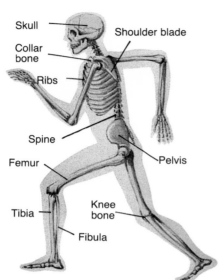

Skull
Shoulder blade
Collar
bone
Ribs
Spine
Femur
Pelvis
Tibia
Knee
bone
Fibula

▲ *The human skeleton is made of a framework of bones that supports the skin, muscles, and other parts.*

▼ *Bones are not solid. They are tubelike, with a hard outer layer protecting a spongy inner layer and a center core of marrow.*

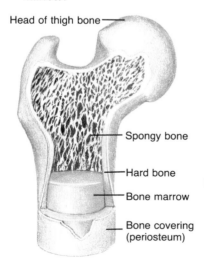

Head of thigh bone
Spongy bone
Hard bone
Bone marrow
Bone covering
(periosteum)

are another native group, few in number but generally wealthy.

Like Bombay's people and culture, its streets are a mixture of the ancient and modern. Cars must stop when cattle decide to rest in the street because these animals are sacred in India. Women may wear *saris*—elegant dresses made from long lengths of cloth—or the latest Paris fashions.

The famous Towers of Silence stand on a hillside. The Parsees leave their dead there to be eaten by vultures. These Parsees are Zoroastrians, followers of a religion started in ancient times in Persia (now Iran). Many Muslims—as well as Christians and Buddhists—live in Bombay.

ALSO READ: ASIA, HINDUISM, INDIA.

BONAPARTE, NAPOLEON see NAPOLEON BONAPARTE.

BONE Like buildings, the bodies of humans and other backboned animals are supported by a firm framework. This framework is made of bone and is called a *skeleton*. The skeleton supports the skin, muscles, and other body parts.

Bone has two main parts—a close, hard outer layer, with an open weblike, spongy part inside. Bone is living tissue, just like other parts of the body.

Young people's bones grow larger along with the rest of the body. Bones stop growing when full growth is reached, usually when a person is 18 to 20 years old. But bone cells continue to be replaced as they wear out. In this way, bone is like other body parts, where worn-out cells are continuously being replaced.

■ LEARN BY DOING

Bone contains calcium and phosphorus. These minerals give bone its hardness. Bone also contains a jellylike substance that gives it some

springiness. Bone can bend somewhat, but it cracks or breaks if the bending force is very strong. Get two chicken leg bones. Soak one in a jar of vinegar for 48 hours. When the soaking time is about up, put the other bone in a pan and heat it in a very hot oven (about 500°F or 260°C) for an hour. When the bone cools, break it. All the soft, jellylike material has been "cooked" out of the bone. Only brittle minerals remain. Take the first bone out of the vinegar and try to break it. What happens? Vinegar dissolved minerals in the bone, leaving it springy. ■

Broken bones normally heal. New bone cells form around the break. The pieces join perfectly when the break is properly set by a doctor.

The bone is like a hard tube. The blood vessels and nerves, which feed and give sensation to the living bone, fit inside the tube, to keep it healthy and let it grow normally. A soft material called *marrow* is also in the center of the tube. Red blood cells are made in the marrow of some bones.

ALSO READ: BLOOD, CELL, FRACTURE, HUMAN BODY, MUSCLE, SKELETON.

BOOK Look around your house and you may see many kinds of books. For example, you may see telephone books, school books, comic books, hobby books, reference books, and many other kinds of books. We use books all the time. But long ago there was no such thing as a book.

Books are one of the oldest ways of recording the things people care about. Throughout the ages, books have recorded what people felt, thought, did, and believed. A book is still a very important way to record things. This encyclopedia, for instance, is one of the most convenient ways to package information. A book can be carried around. It can be easily stored on a shelf. Information in books can be found quickly by using the index or the table of contents.

Paper The invention of paper was the first great advance toward book production. The paper first used was *papyrus*, made from the pith of a reed. Papyrus was used by the Egyptians as early as 4000 B.C. Papyrus came in long sheets that were wrapped around sticks, called *scrolls*. Later animal skins were used to make a material called *parchment*. People learned to make paper from linen pulp in the tenth century A.D. Still later, paper was made from wood pulp.

Printing Books were written by hand until the middle of the 1400's. Then, the printing press was invented and this meant that books could be made faster. Many early books were religious books, such as the Bible.

The first book printed in America was *The Whole Book of Psalms*, published in 1663. Another early American book was *Poor Richard's Almanack*. It was written and printed by Benjamin Franklin, who was a writer and printer before becoming a scientist and statesman.

Much of the work of making a book had to be done by hand even after the printing press was invented. The paper was made by hand. The type, too, was set by hand, and the printing press was operated by hand. The books had to be bound by hand. Making a book was a slow, careful job.

More and more people were learning how to read in the 1800's. More books were needed. New machines were being invented that could produce books faster. A new paper-making machine was invented in 1798 in France. It could make paper in long rolls rather than single sheets. A few years later in Britain, iron printing presses began to replace wooden printing presses.

The Germans began to operate printing presses by steam power instead of by hand about 1811. About 35 years later in America, the type was put into a cylinder, not into a flatbed. The cylinder could revolve and make more impressions in less time than it took to press paper to a flat bed of type. Still later, another American put revolving cylinders of type together with rotating rolls of paper. This made possible the first real mass production of the printed word. In 1884 a machine was invented that could set type. This meant that letters to make words no longer had to be set by hand. By the end of the 19th century, publishers were producing many, many books on all kinds of subjects.

Some books were made in cheap editions with paper covers. They were called "dime novels." This was the beginning of the "paperback book," a very important part of publishing today.

Publishing Book publishing today is a large business. About 51,000 new titles are published each year in the United States, and the number of copies produced amounts to hundreds of millions. About 17,000 U.S. publishers produce books, but only about 300 of these are large companies.

▲ *Roman scrolls were books wrapped around sticks. You unwound the scroll to read the book.*

▼ *A missal or prayer book of the Middle Ages. It looks just like a book of today, but it was written by hand, and each page was beautifully decorated.*

▲ *The Chinese were the first to print books on paper. The earliest known printed book is the* Diamond Sutra, *made around* A.D. *868.*

The most popular book in the history of printing is the Bible.

Book publishing is often divided into *trade books* and *textbooks*. The trade books are so called because they are sold by the bookstore trade. These books include all general interest books sold to the general public—fiction, biographies, poetry, humor, current affairs, and children's books. Textbooks, or educational books, include books for schools, manuals, handbooks, and reference works. More than half the books published in the U.S. are educational.

The book publishing industry is made up of many individuals and companies. Very few publishing firms are large enough to own all the facilities necessary for producing and distributing books. Publishers usually work with many persons. They must deal with writers, copy editors, artists, designers, typesetters, printers, binders, sales personnel, advertisers, and bookstore owners. Book authors usually receive a *royalty*, that is, a percentage of the profit from the sale of each copy of their books.

Producing a Book   Where do books start? Usually, the idea for a book comes from a writer. When an author gets an idea for a book, he or she usually writes a letter to a book editor or publisher and explains the idea. If the editor or publisher thinks the idea is one that will interest readers, the writer is given a contract to write the book. The contract states how much the writer will be paid, how long the book will be, when the book should be completed, and other details.

When publishers receive manuscripts from authors, they make other arrangements for publication of the books. They contact an illustrator to draw the pictures for a book, if it is to have any. They may buy photographs or hire a photographer, if a book is to have special pictures. They hire someone to design a cover and the arrangement of the book, including the size and style of type to be used. They decide on the kind of paper and

select a printer and a binder to produce the book.

Meanwhile, a copy editor goes through the author's manuscript to check for accuracy, grammar, and spelling. When the manuscript is ready, it is turned over to the typesetter, whose work is checked, or *proofread*, before the work is printed and bound. If the book has a hard cover, a protective covering of paper called a *book jacket*, or *dust jacket*, is usually placed on the book. The book jacket is often illustrated and usually has a short description (called a *blurb*) of the contents of the book.

Books are important because they are our chief means of collecting and saving records in a permanent and easily "retrieved" form. Newspapers and magazines are usually thrown away. Radio and television programs are hard to save, even if recorded on tape. Movies, too, are difficult to store in good condition. Expensive equipment is needed to store information on microfilm and computer disks. But books are kept in libraries in every community and institution, and on shelves in almost every home. Because books are permanent, people tend to respect them and become fond of them.

▼ *Pages from an illustrated book on a modern four-color printing press.*

A book is a very personal way of communicating. You can sit down alone with a book. You can read it at your own speed, stopping or starting where you want. That is perhaps why many people say, "Books are friends." In a world of radio, television, motion pictures, computers, and teaching machines, the book is still one of the most important and widely used means of providing information and entertainment.

■ LEARN BY DOING

You can make your own book quite simply. Take ten sheets of paper and fold them in half. Staple them together, or run a string through the fold and tie it. What will be the subject of your book? Fill the pages with your autobiography, perhaps. Write down poems you like—or verse you write yourself. You may want to draw pictures or cut out magazine illustrations to illustrate your book. You may want to design a cover from a pretty color of construction paper and cover the outside. Making your own book gives you a feeling of satisfaction that you have made something different from anyone else's and so truly your own. ■

ALSO READ: COMMUNICATION, LITERATURE, PAPER, PRINTING, PUBLISHING, TYPESETTING.

HAND BOOKBINDING

Endpapers

Sections sewn together

1

Back rounded with hammer

2

3

Cover material

Cover boards

4

Cover material glued on boards

twisted in opposite directions. One side is flat, while the other is rounded, like the top of an airplane wing. The thrower hurls the boomerang forward, giving it a slight twist, which causes it to spin. An expert can make it sail through the air for more than 300 feet (91 m), rise 150 feet (45 m), and then circle several times before returning.

The *non-returning* boomerang is a much deadlier weapon than the return type. It is also larger, heavier, and straighter. An aborigine can kill an enemy with it or bring down a large animal at 500 feet (150 m).

ALSO READ: ABORIGINE, AUSTRALIA.

▲ *Binding a book means putting the pages together and fitting a cover around them. The pages come in sections, like small books. The sections are put in the right order and then sewn together. Glue may be used to fasten the cover and endpapers. Most books are machine-bound, but hand bookbinding is still done occasionally.*

▼ *Throwing a boomerang for sport is fun. But first make sure nobody is in the way!*

BOOKKEEPING see ACCOUNTING AND BOOKKEEPING.

BOOMERANG
The boomerang is a curved wooden throwing stick, used for sport, hunting, and war. The best-known users of boomerangs are the Australian aborigines. But the Hopi Indians of Arizona and primitive peoples in certain parts of India and Africa have also used boomerangs.

The *return* boomerang is used mainly for sport. It is a shallow V-shape, and its arms are slightly

BOONE, DANIEL (1734–1820)
Perhaps the best-known pioneer in American history is Daniel Boone. He lives in the memory of Americans as a great explorer and frontiersman.

Boone grew up on a farm near what is now Reading, Pennsylvania. Friendly Indians in the area taught him many skills for surviving in the wilderness. These skills helped him later when he explored the vast lands across the Allegheny Mountains. Boone made the first of many trips across the mountains to what is now Kentucky in 1769, opening up the land.

Boone blazed the famous Wilderness Road, which was really a trail. It led through the Cumberland Gap, a pass through the Alleghenies. New settlers headed for the lands beyond the Alleghenies over this trail. In 1775, Boone guided a group of settlers into Kentucky and built a stockade and fort. The stockade came under frequent attack from Indians. For months, Boone was held captive by Shawnee raiders and was adopted by their chief. Boone escaped and hurried back to the stockade to aid in its defense. Finally the Indian attacks stopped, and the settlement eventually became the permanent village of Boonesboro.

Boone spent his later years in West Virginia and Missouri. In both places, he worked as a lawmaker and was respected as a man of courage and honesty.

ALSO READ: KENTUCKY, WILDERNESS ROAD.

▲ *Edwin Booth, American actor.*

▼ *John Wilkes Booth, the actor who killed Abraham Lincoln.*

BOOTH FAMILY Booth is a famous name in the history of the American theater. There were three actors named Booth, a father and his two sons. One of the sons, John Wilkes Booth, is best remembered as the man who shot and killed President Abraham Lincoln.

Junius Brutus Booth (1796–1852), the father of this talented family, was born in London, England. In 1821 he came to the United States. Although moody and unstable, he was famed for his superb acting. His greatest roles were in the plays *Richard III* and *Othello*.

His older son, Edwin Thomas Booth (1833–1893), was called the greatest American actor of the 19th century. He and his brother John were born in Bel Air, Maryland. Edwin toured with his father, learning theater craft, and first acted on stage in Boston when he was 15. He later traveled in England and the United

▲ *Daniel Boone, Western pioneer and explorer.*

States, and he won great fame acting in tragic plays. He founded the Players' Club, later a theater museum, in New York.

John Wilkes Booth (1838–1865) began acting at 17. Although the rest of his family sided with the Union in the Civil War, John Wilkes Booth felt sympathy for the South. He became involved in a plot to kill the President, Vice President, and members of the cabinet. On April 14, 1865, he entered a private box in Ford's Theater in Washington, D.C., and shot President Lincoln through the head. Lincoln died the following day. After the shot was fired, Booth leaped down onto the stage, breaking his leg. He managed to escape in spite of stopping to have his leg set by a doctor. Twelve days later he was trapped in a barn in Virginia. The barn was set ablaze, and Booth was killed, either shot by a soldier or by his own hand.

ALSO READ: ACTORS AND ACTING.

BORGIA FAMILY The Borgias sought power in 15th-century Italy through a mixture of intrigue, war, and murder. The family originally lived in Spain, but in 1443 Alfonso de

Borgia went to Italy. In 1455 he became pope as Calixtus III. This good and learned man favored his nephew Rodrigo Borgia (1431–1503), who followed him into the church. But Rodrigo was worldly, ambitious, and ruthless. By bribery and promises made to rivals, he made sure of becoming pope himself, in 1492.

As Alexander VI, Rodrigo was one of the wickedest popes to rule. His main ambition was to advance his own family, for he had several illegitimate children. His son Cesare became a cardinal while in his teens, but left the church to further his worldly power. By 1502 he was master of central Italy. Alexander and Cesare stopped at nothing to gain their ends. If bribery or trickery failed, they tried murder. Poisoning was a favorite method. Cesare may even have poisoned his own father with wine meant for somebody else. Cesare's sister Lucrezia was noted for her great beauty. She married four times to men the Borgias needed as allies. The husbands were got rid of when their usefulness was over.

Borgia power ended with Alexander's death. Lucrezia devoted herself to good works and Cesare died in battle. A great grandson of Alexander, Francisco de Borgia (1510–1572) became a Jesuit missionary and in 1671 was made a saint.

BORNEO Borneo, the world's third largest island (after Greenland and New Guinea) is bigger than the state of Texas. Three-quarters of the land is part of the Republic of Indonesia. Indonesians call the island *Kalimantan*, meaning "river of diamonds." The rest of the island consists of two states of the Federation of Malaysia, Sabah and Sarawak, and the independent sultanate (country ruled by a sultan) of Brunei. (See the map with the article on ASIA.)

Borneo's population includes Malays, Chinese, and tribal peoples. One large tribal group, the Iban or Dyak, once practiced headhunting. As many as 50 Iban families live together in a tribal longhouse. They farm, hunt, and gather wild plants in Borneo's vast forests. More than 50 different kinds of trees grow in these forests. They provide valuable timber, especially teak, and a substance called cutch, used in tanning animal hides. Copper, gold, iron, tin and manganese have all been found in the island. Diamonds occur in many places, but they are slightly yellow in color and not as prized as African diamonds. Rubber and spices, such as cinnamon, cloves, and nutmeg, are exported from Borneo.

Borneo is on the equator and has a wet tropical climate. The average year-round temperature is 80°F (27°C). Some parts of the island get more than 200 inches (5,080 mm) of rain a year.

ALSO READ: MALAYSIA, INDONESIA.

▲ *Lucrezia Borgia was used by her father and brother to help their political intrigues.*

▶ *In Borneo, rubber is grown on small plantations. Here a woman collects latex from a rubber tree. Today, most rubber is made from chemicals in factories and no longer comes from rubber trees.*

▲ *The USS* Constitution, *the Navy's oldest warship, is on permanent exhibition in Boston Harbor.*

▼ *The skyline of Boston, on the bank of the Charles River. Tall buildings, such as the Hancock building, were few in Boston until the 1960's. The city has many old, historic buildings.*

BOSTON Boston, the capital of Massachusetts, is often called the "Hub City." It has been said that Bostonians are so proud of their city that they consider it the *hub*, or center, of the universe. Boston certainly is the hub of New England, being the largest city in the area, and a great center of industry, business, and banking. Boston Harbor has made the city a center of international shipping for centuries. The Boston area has more than a dozen big educational institutions, including Massachusetts Institute of Technology (MIT) and Harvard University, the oldest institution of higher learning in the United States.

Boston was founded ten years after the Pilgrims landed at Plymouth. It was a center of opposition to the British before the American Revolution and was the scene of many important events leading up to it. If you visit the city and follow the Freedom Trail, you can see many historic places. You can go to Paul Revere's house and to the Old North Church, where lanterns were hung to tell Revere if the British were coming by land or by sea. At Boston Harbor you can go aboard the famous fighting ship, *USS Constitution*, better known as "Old Ironsides." You can visit the spots where the Boston Massacre (1770) and the Battle of Bunker Hill (1775) took place.

ALSO READ: AMERICAN REVOLUTION; BOSTON TEA PARTY; MASSACHUSETTS; REVERE, PAUL.

BOSTON MASSACRE The incident Americans call the Boston Massacre was really a riot, or street fight. The fighters were American colonists and British soldiers. The British had decided in 1763 to keep an army in the colonies and to tax the colonists to pay for it. Then the British Parliament passed the Quartering Act in 1765. Colonists had to house British soldiers and give each one candles and five pints of beer a day.

So many British troops were quartered in Boston early in 1770, that the colonists were fed up. Soldiers and colonists traded insults. The situation grew more tense each day. A crowd of about 50 colonists, mostly sailors, teased a lone British sentry on the night of March 5, 1770. They threw snowballs, called him names, and dared him to shoot. Other soldiers came to help, and the crowd jeered at them, too. The soldiers fired into the crowd, killing five colonists and wounding six more.

Crispus Attucks, probably a run-

▼ *The Boston Massacre was one of the key events that hastened the American Revolution.*

away slave and a sailor, was one of the leaders of the colonists at the Boston Massacre. When the soldiers' shots rang out, he was one of the first to die. Samuel Adams, Paul Revere, and other patriots used the "massacre" to fan the flames of revolution.

ALSO READ: ADAMS, SAMUEL; AMERICAN REVOLUTION.

BOSTON TEA PARTY This was one of the events leading up to the American Revolution. It began as a protest by American colonists against unfair British taxes. In 1773 Britain tried to enforce a tax on tea shipped to America from Britain. The colonists refused to drink British tea, or pay the tax. This annoyed the British government, which tried to force the colonies to accept the tea. But when three British tea ships sailed into Boston Harbor, the New Englanders refused to allow the ship to be unloaded. They asked the royal governor to order the tea back to Britain. The governor refused.

A small band of colonists dressed themselves up as Indians, complete with tomahawks, war paint, and feathered headbands. Led by Samuel Adams, they boarded the British ships late at night on December 16, 1773. The "Indians" quickly and qui-

▼ *Disguised as Indians, the protesters boarded the ship and poured its cargo of tea into Boston Harbor.*

etly dumped 340 chests of tea into Boston Harbor. Then they left the ships as silently as they had come and removed all traces of disguise.

This act of rebellion caused great anger in London. The British government decided to teach the colonists a lesson they would not forget. Parliament closed the port of Boston early in 1774. The charter of Massachusetts was revoked. The colonists were forced to let British soldiers live in their homes.

The people of Boston and other colonists were furious. Their fury led to the forming of the First Continental Congress in Philadelphia in September 1774. This meeting united the colonies and was a giant step toward revolution.

ALSO READ: ADAMS, SAMUEL; AMERICAN REVOLUTION; CONTINENTAL CONGRESS.

BOTANICAL GARDEN A botanical garden is like a zoological garden, or zoo, except it is for plants. Many gardens contain plants from all over the world to be studied, bred, and grown. The gardens are usually open for people to come and enjoy the plant "zoo." Some gardens offer educational courses about plants for

Aquatic gardens are made to display and study water plants. Lotus plants from 250-year-old seeds are growing at the Kenilworth Aquatic Gardens in Washington, D.C.

▼ *Botanical gardens grow rare and exotic plants inside large glasshouses. The temperature inside is controlled: moderate for plants from temperate climates, hot for plants from the tropics.*

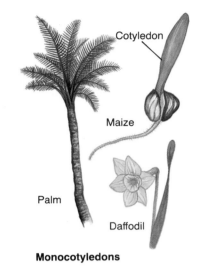

Monocotyledons

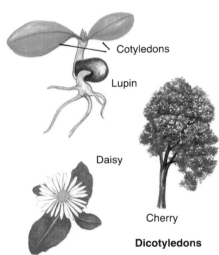

Dicotyledons

▲ *All flowering plants, or* angiosperms, *produce seeds. Some produce one seed leaf, or* cotyledon, *before the true leaves. These plants are called* monocotyledons. *Others produce two seed leaves and are called* dicotyledons.

adults and children. Just walking through a botanical garden can be fascinating, because the plants are usually labeled, and many come from faraway places.

Probably the most famous is the *Royal Botanic Gardens*, located in Kew, England, and sometimes called *Kew Gardens.* This garden was created in 1759. It covers 280 acres (113 hectares). Plants from the entire world are displayed in its gardens and greenhouses. Scientists perform experiments to develop better plants. Some of the research on rubber trees planted there has helped the rubber industry.

The New York Botanical Garden, located in New York City, covers 235 acres (95 hectares). It has sent out many expeditions (searching parties) looking for new plants. Scientists from this garden have found thousands of new kinds of plants. They also conduct research to produce stronger plants, to control plant disease, and to find medical uses for plants.

Botanical gardens are also located in Brooklyn, New York; Washington, D.C.; and St. Louis, Missouri. The St. Louis garden has plants from all parts of the world.

There are botanical gardens in other countries, too. The garden in Hamilton, Ontario, Canada, is near McMaster University. It has a famous rock garden. There is also a botanical garden in Montreal, Quebec. The lovely Jardin des Plantes is located in Paris, France.

Botanical gardens where trees, shrubs, and other woody plants are grown under natural conditions are called *arboretums.* Scientists working in arboretums have grown new kinds of trees and learned how to cure many tree diseases. Most arboretums are open to the public. They are good examples of the beauty of landscaped (arranged for best effect) gardens. There are trial sections in most arboretums where experiments in raising

new and unusual trees are carried out. Some of the best known are the Morton Arboretum at Lisle, Illinois, near Chicago; the Arnold Arboretum in Boston; and the National Arboretum in Washington, D.C.

ALSO READ: GARDENING, PLANT, PLANT BREEDING.

BOTANY Botany is the science or study of plants, but long before it ever became a science people realized the importance of learning about plants. Early peoples roamed about in search of wild roots, berries, and seeds for food. By trial and error, they learned which plants were good to eat and which were poisonous. They also found out which were best for making clothing, houses, and tools. They discovered that the juices of some plants could be used as medicines.

In time, people began also to wonder about the secrets of plant life. How do plants grow? Do they need food the way people do? What makes some plants sicken and die? What allows certain plants to grow only in water, while others grow on land? The philosophers of ancient Greece tried to answer thousands of such questions. Theophrastus, a pupil of Aristotle in ancient Greece, was one of the first to organize his study of plants in a scientific way. He is known as the "father of botany."

Botanists of the 1500's were especially interested in the healing powers of plants. Information about plants used in medicine was collected in the books called *herbals.* The people who wrote them were called *herbalists.* They made important contributions to the science of botany by describing and drawing pictures of hundreds of plants. But not all their ideas were correct. For example, they believed that a leaf shaped like a heart could be used to cure heart disease.

Today, so much is known about plants—and so much has yet to be learned—that one botanist could never hope to study it all. That is why botanists usually concentrate on just one branch of botany.

Plant taxonomy is the science of naming and classifying plants. Plant taxonomists must study different plants to see how they are alike and how they are different. Then they can group them into different categories. The great Swedish botanist Carolus Linnaeus began the modern system of plant classification.

Plant morphology is the study of the form and structure of plant organs—roots, stems, leaves, flowers, fruits, and seeds.

Plant cytology is the study of plant cells. Robert Hooke, an English scientist, discovered the cell in 1665 while studying a piece of cork under a microscope.

Plant physiology is the study of what plants do and how they behave. Physiologists can tell you what makes flowers open and close, or what causes certain plants to lean toward light. They also study how plants make their food and how plants use air, light, water, and minerals.

Plant pathology is the study of plant diseases. Most of these are caused by bacteria, viruses, fungi, or small animals that get into the plants. Some are caused by a lack of certain minerals in the soil. A plant pathologist tries to find the causes and cures of plant diseases.

Plant ecology is the study of how plants fit into their natural environment. It involves studying how they are affected by soil and climate and by neighboring plants and animals, and also how the plants themselves affect their surroundings. Plant ecologists try to find out exactly what conditions each kind of plant requires. These scientists are also very involved with the conservation of rare plants, making sure that they are given just the right conditions for healthy growth in nature reserves and in botanic gardens.

Plant genetics is the study of how plants give characteristics to their offspring. Gregor Mendel, an Austrian monk, pioneered in this field with his experiments with garden peas. Knowledge of genetics helps botanists grow new breeds of plants that combine the best features of several varieties. Many of today's quick-growing and high-yield crop plants have been produced in this way.

■ LEARN BY DOING

You can be a "part-time" botanist by growing a seed until it blossoms and produces seeds again. Kidney beans are good, because they grow well and quickly. Use a medium-sized flower pot and rich soil. Plant the seeds and place the pot in a sunny window. Keep the soil moist, but do not let it become sticky or waterlogged. Things to discover. (1) How many leaves are there on the seedling? (2) How does the plant change as new leaves appear? (3) How long before flowers appear? (4) What are the seed pods like? (5) How many seeds are there inside? Keep a weekly record of your plant's progress. ■

ALSO READ: BIOLOGY; BURBANK, LUTHER; CELL; ECOLOGY; FLOWER; GENETICS; LINNAEUS, CAROLUS; MENDEL, GREGOR; PLANT; PLANT BREEDING; PLANT KINGDOM.

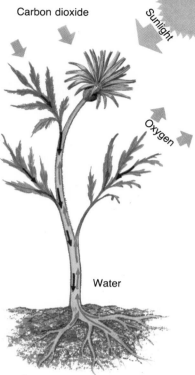

Carbon dioxide · Sunlight · Oxygen · Water

▲ *A plant uses water plus sunlight energy and carbon dioxide from the air to make sugar and starch (for food). At the same time, the plant gives off oxygen.*

▼ *The base of a flower is the attached to a swollen base, or* receptacle. *The green* sepals *protect the bud containing the* petals. *Inside are the reproductive organs:* stamens *(male) and* carpels *(female).*

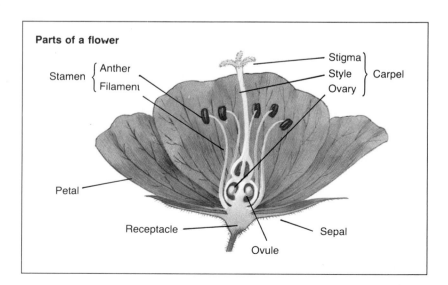

Parts of a flower

Stamen { Anther, Filament · Stigma · Style · Ovary } Carpel · Petal · Receptacle · Ovule · Sepal

▲ *Cattle herding in Botswana. In this African country, cattle are a major source of farm income. Often children help to herd the cattle.*

BOTSWANA The name Botswana means "land of the Tswana people." This African country, which lies far from the sea, is bordered by Zimbabwe, the Republic of South Africa, and Namibia (South West Africa). (See the map with the article on AFRICA.)

A vast highland covers most of the country. There are hills 5,000 feet (1,500 m) high in the east and southeast. Near them the great Kalahari Desert spreads over southwestern Botswana. Swamplands around the Okovango River abound with wildlife. Fertile areas in the northern and eastern parts of the country supply most of the food.

Botswana's climate is hot and dry: summer temperatures can rise to 100° F (37.8°C). Droughts (long periods without rain) are common in Botswana. There is little cultivated farmland. Most people keep herds of cattle, some of great size. Many of the young men leave Botswana to work in mines in neighboring countries. At Orapa and Jwaneng, within Botswana, are two of the world's largest diamond mines. Diamonds, and other minerals that have been discovered, are bringing wealth to this poor country.

Botswana is about the size of Texas but has no large cities. Most of the people speak Bantu languages. English, however, is the official language of Botswana. Many village people live in round houses made of hardened mud with thatched roofs. Some are Christians, but most practice tribal religions.

Bushmen were the original inhabitants of Botswana. They still live in the hot Kalahari Desert, much as they did thousands of years ago. They hunt game with poisoned arrows and dig up wild plants. They speak an unusual language, Khoisan, which includes clicking sounds. In 1885 the country, then called Bechuanaland (after the local people, the Bechuana) came under British control. Bechuanaland was a British colony until it became independent in 1966 and changed its name to Botswana.

Botswana is ruled by a National Assembly, which elects a president. A House of Chiefs advises the government on laws affecting the tribes.

ALSO READ: AFRICA.

BOTTLE see GLASS, PACKAGING.

BOTSWANA

Capital City: Gaborone (95,000 people).

Area: 224,706 square miles (581,987 sq. km).

Population: 1,220,000.

Government: Republic.

Natural Resources: Diamonds, nickel, copper, coal, salt, cattle.

Export Products: Diamonds, copper, meat, hides and skins, textiles.

Unit of Money: Pula.

Official Language: English.